THE CEO OF SELF

THE CEO OF SELF:
AN EXECUTIVE FUNCTIONING WORKBOOK

JAN JOHNSTON-TYLER, MA

Printed in the United States of America

First Printing, June 2014

ISBN: 978-1499294934
LCCN: 2014910340

EvoLibri Consulting
www.evolibri.com
media@evolibri.com

Cover Design, Graphics, and Typesetting by Jan Johnston-Tyler
Edited by Trish Thorpe

Organizing is what you do before you do something so that when you do it, it is not all mixed up.

– A. A. Milne

Table of Contents

Preface...

About This Book

<u>Section I</u>

What Executive Functioning Is ...And Is Not

Time Management

Section II

Project Management

Information Management

Thought Management

Obstacle Management

On Becoming the CEO of Self

Bibliography

Appendix

THE CEO OF SELF

Preface...

Everyone is busier now than before. We know it, we say it, we feel it, and most of us seem to believe it. And yet, there is no sign of slowing down. In fact, everything seems to be whirring past us in a blur: the demise of family dinners, constant multitasking, late-night catch up for work and school, a never-ending list of things to get done, all vie for our attention.

And yet, no matter how many more gadgets we buy, no matter how well-synced we are, we are perpetually looking for better ways to organize ourselves and be even more efficient. As stated in *Busier Than Ever! Why American Families Can't Slow Down*, "people [are] frequently preoccupied with how they should manage or organize their work and family obligations."[1] Sound familiar? Even those of us with exceptional time management and organizational skills—major components of what we call executive function skills—are constantly looking for ways to do more, with less—and to do it faster.

Kids are certainly not immune from this pressure either. In our school district, Kindergartners get homework packets each week, middle schoolers typically have two or more hours of homework each night, and high school students frequently have four or more hours of homework each night—and six hours a day, including weekends, is not uncommon. This, on top of chores at home, extracurricular activities, sports, and family obligations. No wonder so many of our kids feel stressed and overwhelmed—and heaven forbid that our child has a learning disability, Asperger's Syndrome/autism, ADHD, or another challenge that impairs executive functioning. How can they ever survive in this lightning-fast society?

---

1   Darrah, C., Freeman, J., English-Lueck, J. (2007). *Busier than ever! Why American families can't slow down.* Stanford University Press, Stanford, CA, pp. 248-249.

As Stephen P. Hinshaw, noted expert on ADHD, states in his latest book:

> *The more we push young children to become fast learners in school at ever-earlier ages—and the more that adults are valued for their performance and productivity in a ruthlessly competitive global workplace—the more than individual differences in attention, inhibitory control, and self-regulation will stand out.* [2]

The truth is, our lives have gotten more and more complex over the last few decades, and it has gotten harder and harder for adults—let alone children and teens—to stay on top of everything we need to get done in a given day.

And even though we have access to amazing technology that makes organization, information retrieval, and day-to-day productivity much easier, there is a downside—the faster we get, the more we seem to be expected to do. Between 2003 and 2008, roughly 50% of working Americans brought work home because they could not complete it during the normal workday. [3] Modern day business workers have felt this push for more, more, more in the mantra work smarter, not harder, a quote which is attributed, perhaps ironically, to Scrooge McDuck, the tight-fisted, mean-spirited, exploitative uncle of Disney's Donald Duck.

And the evidence shows we have done just that—worked smarter to be sure, but perhaps harder as well. According to the Bureau of Labor and Statistics (BLS), American productivity more than doubled in the decades between 1980-1990 and 2000-2007, [4] as measured in units of output per hour, a theoretic unit of productivity the BLS uses in calculating worker productivity.

Clearly, technology has had a great deal to do with our productivity increase—to gain double the productivity in just a quarter of a century is astounding. But this is fairly old news—as stated in Businessweek almost ten years ago, "[o]ver the past 25 years, the Information Revolution has boosted productivity by almost 70%." [5] But technology may not be the entire reason for this increase. According to the US Census, our average working hours, which steadily decreased between 1950 and 1970, perhaps in part to the much-heralded time-saving devices such as dishwashers and microwave ovens,

---

2   Hinshaw, S. P. and R. Scheffler (2014). The ADHD Explosion: Myths, Medication, Money, and Today's Push for Performance. Oxford University Press, New York, NY. pp. 31.

3   Pabilonia, S. and L. Eldridge (2010). Bringing work home: Implications for BLS productivity measures. *Monthly Labor Review*, 133 (12), pp. 18-35.

4   Bureau of Labor and Statistics. Productivity change in the nonfarm business sector, 1947-2011. Average annual percent change. http://www.bls.gov/lpc/prodybar.htm, retrieved February 8, 2012.

5   The Real Reasons You're Working So Hard… and what you can do about it Businessweek, October 3, 2005. Retrieved February 8, 2012.

have steadily increased since 1980, at the start of the technology revolution.[6] Clearly then, we are working harder as well.

The question is—can we double American worker productivity again in the next 25 years? Do we want to? Will our teachers and employers expect us to, and will it mean more hours on the job, in the classroom, or doing work activities from home in our leisure hours? It's hard to know what the future will bring, but we can be certain that being more organized and productive in the hours we dedicate to school and work will make us more efficient, and thus, give us more leisure time in our days, no matter how short those days may become. And, who knows what the 'next big thing' in our technological future may allow us to accomplish in a 24-hour period.

But, we also know that technology today—in the form of information overload—can actually make us more scattered and inefficient. More things are vying for our attention, making it harder and harder to stay on task with text messages chiming, voicemails blinking, emails dinging, and social media updates to read. And once we succumb to checking our communication channels, we are that more likely to succumb to the siren call of our favorite fan site, YouTube, or one quick game, be it Scrabble™ or World of Warcraft, and as any teenager can tell you, the time just slips away and 'suddenly' it's 2 am.

Many of us are hooked on our constant contact with the virtual world—why else would a sane person attempt to text someone while driving? Internet addiction, also called Problematic Internet Use (PIU), represents a rapidly growing cause of concern in mental health workers, colleges, and parents alike, and some mental health professionals believe that it should be classified as a true psychological disorder in the Diagnostic and Statistical Manual of Mental Disorders,[7] as a separate, standalone diagnosis.

The truth is, increasing productivity, perhaps even enhancing executive functioning, exists on a fine edge between getting more done and becoming obsessively organized and connected to the world beyond, which in turn can reduce our productivity. It is indeed a cautionary tale.

While there are no miracles, there certainly is hope, whether you are a corporate executive looking for ways to improve your performance at work, a busy parent trying to keep your family on track, a college student with ADHD or a learning disorder

---

6   Rones, Philip L., Randy E. Ilg, and Jennifer M. Gardner (1997). Trends in hours of work since the mid-1970's. *Monthly Labor Review* April: 3- 14.

7   Shapira, N., et al. (2003). Problematic Internet Use: Proposed Classification and Diagnostic Criteria. *Depression and Anxiety Journal*, pp. 17:207–216.

finishing your degree, or a teacher helping a middle school child with Asperger's Syndrome. The world is unlikely to slow down any time soon, and those individuals who have an edge will be the ones who can more effectively manage all aspects of their lives—time, space, and even their thoughts—and who can "see these behaviors as a unified, interrelated set of practices."[8] In short, those individuals who can master the various aspects of executive functioning—the individuals who can become effective Chief Executive Officers of their lives.

The skills outlined in this workbook can be learned by teens, young and older adults, including those with and without learning difficulties. All it takes is a little time and effort, which will be handsomely rewarded with less chaos, more free time, and most

importantly, a sense of calm in a very busy world. Don't we all deserve that?

...and Acknowledgements

Books like this get written for one reason—to help other people with their lives. So first, I would like to thank all of my clients who have helped make this book a reality, because without them, I would never have thought programmatically about what makes executive functioning so important, and how to remediate these skills in those to whom they do not come naturally. It is truly a blessing to do work that we love— and I truly love my work.

This book is, like most, a labor of love. I have decided to self-publish it, rather than to go through my previous publisher, in hopes that I can get it into your hands sooner, and with less fuss. The subject matter is timely, and it is important to me to get this information out as soon as I can. To that end, all errors and omissions are my own.

Books do not get written and published without support, and to that end, I would like to thank Maia for always making me smile, Will for showing me that with help and patience we can all succeed, and to Joedy for keeping me sane each and every day. Without the three of you, my life would indeed be empty.

Finally—throughout this book you'll notice that 'things happen for a reason'— meaning, we often make forward motion because of the work we have done in the past. It may look like luck, and maybe it is, but often it's a matter of timing and learning how to see opportunities in any given situation.

8   Darrah, C., Freeman, J., English-Lueck, J. (2007). *Busier than ever! Why American families can't slow down.* Stanford University Press, Stanford, CA, pp. 248-249.

To that end, I'm grateful that my dear friend Trish Thorpe returned to the Bay Area when she did, as she has edited this book for me, and helped me get it off to press. No amount of coffee and dinners can repay her for her help. I could not have done this without her.

About This Book

This book can be used either as a study guide by an individual or as a workbook as part of a leader-led class. The intention is to use this book mindfully—that it to say, learn about a set of skills, reflect on how these skills can be applied to your daily life, and then start using them. Learners can go through the book chapter after chapter straight through, or they work on one chapter, and put the book down and pick it up again later, learning about a new topic, applying the information, and then take a break. Additionally, it may be helpful to return to a specific section at a later time and review and rework the exercises.

This book is divided into two parts—the first part covers basic executive functioning skills that are required in late adolescence and through adulthood. These skills should be covered in the given sequence, and should be learned before moving on to the second part of the book:

❑ **Time Management**—Time is frequently our most important commodity, and as such, it's where we start the conversation of executive functioning skills. In this chapter, readers will learn what their normal daily rhythms are, why calendars are important and what type to use, how we can all be more conscious about how we spend our time, and several tips on how to 'multi-task' and manage our time more effectively. We will also cover how sensory challenges can interfere with time management.

❑ **Space Management**—Next to time, the next biggest challenge in executive functioning is how we manage our physical space. Readers will learn why it matters where we put things, and why a reasonably clean work environment is pivotal to being effective. We will also discuss several methods to use to keep our physical space free from excessive clutter.

❑ **Memory Management**—Although working memory is discussed in previous chapters as the linchpin to our executive functioning system overall, this chapter goes into more depth on the topic. Here, you will learn how memory works, as well as different ways to increase memory retention when studying or learning a new skill.

The second part of this book contains more advanced executive functioning topics that can be learned once the basics have been covered:

❑ **Project Management**—In this chapter, you will learn that nearly every multi-step task we undertake is in fact a project, and thus could benefit from simple project management tools. The learner will develop his or her own mission statement, and learn how goals and objectives flow from that mission in a top-down fashion, and how goals and objectives can be used to develop actionable tasks. We will also discuss the SMART model (Specific, Measurable, Actionable, Realistic, and Timebound).

❑ **Information Management**—As a follow-up to project management, this chapter goes into more detail on how to develop a workable project plan, teaching the learner how to evaluate information using different criteria based on relatedness, validity to task, and overall importance. We will also expose the learner to concepts such as sequencing and dependencies.

❑ **Thought Management**—This chapter departs somewhat from pragmatics, and discusses some of the ways in which we all derail ourselves through negative thinking. Going over some basic principles of Cognitive Behavioral Therapy, this chapter helps uncover some common ways we go down rat holes, and demonstrates ways to reframe situations in more positive ways.

❑ **Obstacle Management**—In the final chapter, learners will explore ways to identify when they have hit a wall—and what to do. We will discuss how to avoid crises in the first place, discuss the difference between perseverance and perseveration, and learn when it makes sense to give up, keep going, or reframe.

Language & Typographical Conventions

This book is intended to be easy to read and use, and thus the tone of this book is intended to be informal. I, for one, have read far too many difficult texts and articles in search of useful information, and I have endeavored to write a book that is readable, and occasionally enjoyable. It makes no sense to write in a form that is not accessible to its audience!

1. To the extent possible, I have also tried to make this book gender-neutral, which means that I use my own construct of 's/he' for he or she, and occasionally (and consciously incorrectly) use 'they' or 'their' instead of s/he or 'his or her.'

2. I have used bold to identify new concepts or terms and italics to denote sample names and to denote emphasis.

3. I have used callout boxes throughout the book which contain useful tips or background information that supports the main text. You can find these in the Table of Contents as **ThoughtBoxes**.

4. Finally, I have used some abbreviations in this book, including:

    ❑ **EF** for executive functioning
    ❑ **LD** for learning disability
    ❑ **ASD** for autistic spectrum disorder
    ❑ **ADHD** for attention deficit

THE CEO OF SELF

What Executive Functioning Is...And Is Not

This workbook is about how to increase your executive functioning abilities, but before we start, it's a good idea to describe what executive functioning is. Let's start with the definition from *The American Heritage Medical Dictionary*:

ex•ec•u•tive function

n.

The cognitive process that regulates an individual's ability to organize thoughts and activities, prioritize tasks, manage time efficiently, and make decisions.[1]

So, executive functioning (or EF for short) is essentially how we get things done—how we organize our thoughts to remember that we need to go to the dentist, how we make the decision to call the dentist for an appointment, how we get to the dentist on time, and how we remember where we put the insurance card we need to take to the dentist.

In short, EF is responsible for helping us do pretty much everything we consciously choose to do—we don't need EF to do automatic (or, more accurately, autonomic) things like breathing or blinking. But we do need EF to do many of the conscious acts we perform every day—preparing a special family meal, choosing what to wear to work on a hot day, buying a perfect birthday present for our best friend.

---

1   The American Heritage® Medical Dictionary Copyright © 2007, 2004 by Houghton Mifflin Company. Published by *Houghton Mifflin Company*. Accessed online from Freeonline Dictionary, February 21, 2012. http://medical-dictionary.thefreedictionary.com/executive+function.

Given that definition, the majority of us have a pretty effective chief executive officer, or set of executive functioning skills—why would we need to improve? As it happens, executive function can be seen as existing on a continuum. On one side, there is very little EF—we put a block of cheese on the table with a loaf of bread and call it a meal. On the other side, we spend all day preparing a lavish meal, set a gorgeous table replete with silver and fresh flowers and place cards, and choose an exceptional wine to serve with dinner. Most of us live somewhere between the EF opposites of 'Caveman' and 'Perfect Host(ess)', and that's just where we should be.

But, if we find ourselves constantly late for appointments, unable to find our keys or cell phone a couple of times a week, unable to keep on top of our bills or homework, living in unbearable clutter, completely stymied when we sit down to our computer to do our work—we may need additional executive functioning skills to make our lives run more smoothly. And, even if our personal CEO works well now, learning new skills and techniques can only make us more effective now and in the future.

So, what are the specific areas of executive functioning? Here's another definition of EF:

> Executive function is an umbrella term for cognitive processes such as planning, working memory, attention, problem solving, verbal reasoning, inhibition, mental flexibility, multi-tasking, initiation and monitoring of actions.[2]

While there is discussion about what the exact components are of Executive Functioning, the definition above is fairly all-encompassing, and provides a good foundation for what we'll be discussing in this book. Our cognitive processes, at their best, work in concert with one another in a never-ending symphony that gets us though each and every day, and together our cognitive processes are the rough equivalent of our human operating system. Individually, they provide the distinct functions described below.

❑ Our **Planning Ability** helps us organize our activities toward specific goals. Making dinner requires that we bought groceries, got items out of the cupboards and refrigerator, maybe looked up a recipe, prepared and served the food. Without the ability to project a need or desire in the future (hunger) and then sequence events (going shopping before starting dinner), our we cannot meet our goals (dinner). This is how we plan.

2   Chan, R. C. K., Shum, D., Toulopoulou, T. and Chen, E. Y. H. (2008). Assessment of executive functions: Review of instruments and identification of critical issues. *Archives of Clinical Neuropsychology.* 2 23 (2): 201-216.

❑ **Working Memory** is like our CPU and flash memory combined—it provides some processing power (how our brain understands what we see, feel, etc.) and the storage of information. The memory component is like our web browser's cache—it keeps information handy so that it can be readily 'downloaded' without too much searching through our brain's database, so that the processing can happen faster. If I'm standing in the produce aisle and thinking about whether I have lettuce in the frige at home, I am using my working memory.

❑ Our **Attentional System** allows us to focus on the task at hand. Many of us have lapses in attention, some with disastrous results. If I am yakking on my cell phone while I'm pushing a cart through the supermarket and crash into a display of oranges, it's probably because I was not focused on the task at hand—namely, driving the shopping cart. Note that our attentional systems can be very easily interrupted by distraction—a blinking icon on our computer screen, someone talking, an itchy sweater, even our own thoughts, can all interrupt our attention. On the opposite side of the attentional spectrum, some people who have difficulty focusing on some tasks can focus like a laser beam on other tasks that they particularly like or are good at (a preferred task). This phenomenon is frequently referred to as hyperfocus[3] or 'the flow' (a term coined by noted positive psychologist, Mihaly Csikszentmihalyi) and is common with writers, artists, and (not surprisingly) gamers.

❑ **Multi-tasking** is related to our attentional system, in that none of us actually multi-task, but do several things in very quick succession, alternating our attentional focus from one task to another.[4] As it turns out, then, high-functioning 'attentional software' not only keeps us focused when necessary, but can pull our focus off the task we are currently working on and move it to the next task we need to do—sometimes in very rapid succession. This appears to be the opposite of hyperfocus, where nearly all of a person's attention is on one thing alone. Think back to the shopping cart—if I am so focused on getting lettuce for dinner, I am oblivious to the fact that there is someone careening around a corner in front of me, or that the fire alarm in the building has gone off and everyone is running to the door. Now, if I am multi-tasking while I am shopping, my primary focus is on driving the cart safely to the produce aisle with intermittent task reminders that the goal is lettuce. Of course, multi-

3   M. Weiss, L. Trokenberg Hechtman, and G. Weiss (1999). ADHD in adulthood: A guide to current theory, diagnosis, and treatment. The John Hopkins University Press, Baltimore, Maryland, pp. 52.
4   E. Ophir, C. Nass, and AD. Wagner (2009). Cognitive control in media multitaskers. Proceedings of the National Academy of Sciences, PNAS August 24, 2009; published online before print www.pnas.org_cgi_doi_10.1073_pnas.0903620106; accessed January 25th, 2012.

tasking has various levels of complexity, and thankfully most of us can easily navigate a shopping trip without creating Armageddon in the aisles.

❑ Many people would say that **Problem Solving** is an art rather than a skill, but the basic tools needed to solve a problem are related to our EF system. In its most basic form, a problem occurs when we are working on a given task and then for some reason we cannot complete it the way we had intended. We are momentarily stuck and we must choose a new path to complete our task, or we must decide that our task cannot be completed. Back to the grocery store. I had planned on making Caesar Salad for dinner, but they are out of romaine lettuce, its main ingredient. I'm stuck. What do I do? I can have a hissy fit with the store manager, or I can decide that I just won't make dinner, period, because my plans or ruined. Or I can solve the problem. My choices are to go to another store and see if they have romaine or change my menu to another type of salad. Good problem solving may take years to master, and it may be inhibited by our own negative thoughts ("I can't do this, dinner is ruined.")

❑ **Verbal Reasoning** is our ability to understand and respond to—or process— both written and spoken language. This processing exists both at a basic level, such as following a simple instruction ("Could you please reach that loaf of bread for me?") to more difficult processes such as reading, conversational or public speaking, and multi-step instructions ("Go to the farmer's market, and find the guy who sells the Heirloom tomatoes. Ask him if..."). Note-taking in school or business is probably one of the most difficult tasks we do which calls on our verbal reasoning. We must attend to the lecturer, understand and synthesize what s/he is saying, reframe the content in our own words, and then write our version of the information down, all nearly-simultaneously. Not surprisingly, this is a difficult task for those with Central Auditory Processing or Attentional disorders. Even those of us without a learning disorder can get overwhelmed when what we are trying to do strains this sub-system, which is why most of us cannot write and speak at the same time, as both tasks are forms of expressive language.

❑ **Inhibition** is not just about wearing clothes at the supermarket, though remembering to get dressed would definitely be part of your executive functioning system overall. Our inhibition system in terms of EF can be thought of as the split-second decision to not react when our brain encounters internal or external stimuli. Let's say someone passes me in the grocery store whom I know has said vicious and untrue things about a friend. I absolutely loathe this person, and part of me would love to trip him and watch him fall flat on his face—and I even think about doing that as he passes me by. But, the rational, calm part of me tells me "Stop!" and I let this person simply pass me without harm. Inhibition is what stops us from scratching our privates in public, from yelling obscenities at a teacher or boss, and so forth. It is the thin line between our animalistic tendencies and our socialized selves.

❑ **Mental Flexibility** is the "...ability to shift to a different thought or action according to changes in a situation".[5] Mental flexibility is required for good problem solving, but is also necessary for the creative process, brainstorming, being able to see both sides to a given situation, and 'thinking out of the box.' For example, if I were stuck in the produce aisle with no romaine for my Caesar Salad, mental flexibility might tell me that I could try to make a new and different kind of Caesar Salad using butter lettuce instead of romaine.

❑ **Initiation**, also known as activation[6] or intrinsic motivation, is a key area of concern in EF, and is frequently noted in individuals with ADHD[7] and depression.[8] Without a sense of initiation, life itself is very difficult. We don't have the motivation to make plans, clean the house, do our homework, or pretty much anything. Without initiation, I may know that I need to go grocery shopping and maybe cook a meal, but I probably won't get off the couch to go do it. Much has been written about how to increase motivation, and the most common solution is to create a system of rewards or consequences to get an individual (or ourselves) moving. We'll talk about that later!

❑ **Monitoring of Actions** is necessary to keep all of our activities moving in concert toward one or more goals. If we are at the supermarket with the intent of buying ingredients for dinner, and we suddenly get caught up in apples, and decide that it would be interesting to create a spreadsheet with information on the different kinds—color, taste, price—and completely forget that we were there to buy groceries for our dinner, then our action monitor isn't working. We all need a way to monitor our own performance against goals that we or others have set, or we are unlikely to get anything but the most minimal tasks done. [9]

Executive Functioning skills really are the system software we all need to get things done in our lives. Without them, or with severe deficits in one or more areas, it

---

5   Hill, Elisabeth L. (2004). Executive dysfunction in autism. *Trends in Cognitive Sciences,* 8 (1), pp. 26-32.

6   Brown, T. (2001). *Brown Attention-Deficit Disorder Scales®* [Measurement instrument]. Pearson Publishing, San Antonio, TX.

7   R. Barkley (2000). Excerpts from Lecture in San Francisco, June 17, 2000, published by permission by SchwabLearning.org, Charles and Helen Schwab Foundation, pp. 25.

8   van Reekum R, Stuss DT, and Ostrander L. (2005). Apathy: why care? *Journal of Neuropsychiatry & Clinical Neurosciences,* 17, pp. 7-19.

9   Cooper-Kahn, J. and Dietzel, L. (2008). *Late, Lost, and Unprepared.* Woodbine House, Bethesda, MD. pp 9-17.

is difficult to navigate the world around us in an effective way. The good news is that nearly all of us can increase our own EF effectiveness with a little work and perseverance, which is why you bought this book. It really can be done, and the skills you learn here can serve you for the rest of your life.

However, we all should be aware that there is no easy panacea or fix-all for the increasing demands and major distractions that students and workers face to increase their productivity. While it's unlikely that teachers and corporations will see another 100% increase in productivity in the next 25 years without another major shift in technology like the personal computer and the internet, we all need to learn to make good choices about how we allocate our precious resources of time and energy. Executive functioning cannot add more hours to the day, or radically increase productivity unless we have another massive change such as those technologies have brought us in the last few decades.

So, how will you spend your precious resources? We have choices each and every day if we only stopped to think. We can continue to be overwhelmed, stressed, and ineffective, or we can learn to manage all aspects of our lives more efficiently. It's time to become chief executive officers of our own lives. Let's get started!

Section I

Time Management

Space Management

Virtual Management

Memory Management

Time Management

Let's start by talking about time. Time can be our friend or our enemy, it depends on how you look at it, and how you use it. In fact, the best way to manage anxiety for busy people may not be to relax more—but to manage their time better. Time management is very difficult for many people—you are not alone! The difference between you and those who successfully manage time are a few simple tools.

Identifying What's Important

Before we can figure out how to manage your time, we need to figure out what you want to be spending your time on. Below, list seven priorities that are vital you do every week—and don't forget to include downtime and social activities.

My Seven Important Things	Hours Spent	Hours Needed
1		
2		
3		
4		
5		
6 *Downtime*		
7 *Social life*		
Totals Per Week:		

Okay, go back to your "seven priorities" list, and estimate how many hours a week you spend on each activity and total them up. Finally, really think about how much time you actually need to do each activity as you would like. Is there a difference between the time you need and the time you actually have? Don't worry, we'll get to that later. Also remember that this list might change—there are times in our lives when we have something important to work on that is time-bound such as getting ready for a special event. Other items that we do most every day may also be of greater or lesser importance throughout our lives—you might be taking some really hard classes right now, or work might be especially easy this week, so it's a good idea to revisit this list a few times a year or at the start of a new school term, job, or major life event.

Time Budgeting

Once you have an idea of how much time you need to do the things that are important to you, we can balance the time needed across the time available. We do this by simply writing it all down in a weekly view. Now, it's true that every week is going to be a little different. And no, by writing things down doesn't mean that the world will stop spinning on its axis, but it is important to visualize how you spend your time.

	Morning	Midday	Afternoon	Early PM	Late PM
	6-10	10-2	2-6	6-10	10-2
Sunday					
Monday					
Tuesday					
Wednesday					
Thursday					
Friday					
Saturday					

Now, looking at this calendar—did you get all seven priorities scheduled in the week? Is there enough time to do each one to your satisfaction? If so, you're golden—you have a well-balanced calendar. If you didn't find time, don't panic!

Chunking Work

We're going to go back for a second and look at your original list of seven items—were any of them big 'chunks' of generic activities like 'work' or 'homework' or 'housework?'

If so, there's a good chance that you may need to break down those chunks into manageable tasks. For example, if one of your chunks is indeed 'homework,' and if you faithfully do your homework every day as listed on your time budget calendar, does that mean that all of your homework will be done at the end of the week? No. There's a very good chance that you will spend the majority of your time working on the homework that you actually like to do (or dislike less) and that the truly loathsome work will never actually get done. And, you will be able to say and completely truthfully—I worked 30 hours (or, whatever) on homework this last week, and I still can't get to my Jacobean Dramatic Arts homework (or, whatever). Funny how that works, isn't it?

So, in order to be completely successful in this endeavor, you need to be honest here: *Will I do a complete job of all related tasks if I don't list them out separately?* If the answer is yes, that's great. You don't need to break down the task. If, however, you are immobilized with uncertainty about where to begin, or if you always manage to 'not have time' for one or more task then you'll need to chunk the task into manageable pieces. Here are a few sample ways of breaking things down into manageable chunks:

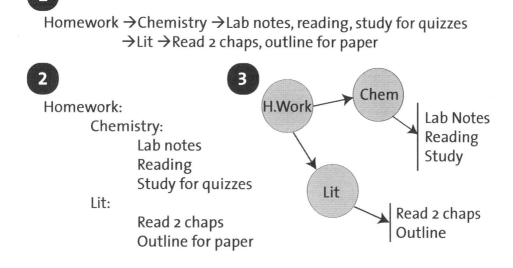

1

Homework →Chemistry →Lab notes, reading, study for quizzes
→Lit →Read 2 chaps, outline for paper

2

Homework:
    Chemistry:
        Lab notes
        Reading
        Study for quizzes
    Lit:
        Read 2 chaps
        Outline for paper

3

H.Work → Chem → Lab Notes / Reading / Study
H.Work → Lit → Read 2 chaps / Outline

So, in the box on the next page, take your 'larger' tasks and break them down to their individual components, using one of the methods above, or another method of your choosing.

BREAKING IT DOWN

Daily Energy Rhythms

Next, we're going to do another exercise that may seem completely unrelated to calendaring (but really isn't, of course). On the following chart, let's map out what your energy levels are throughout the day by placing an X on the grid for each intersection that indicates about how you typically feel at that time on a regular school or work day, and then connect the Xs to see your daily rhythm.

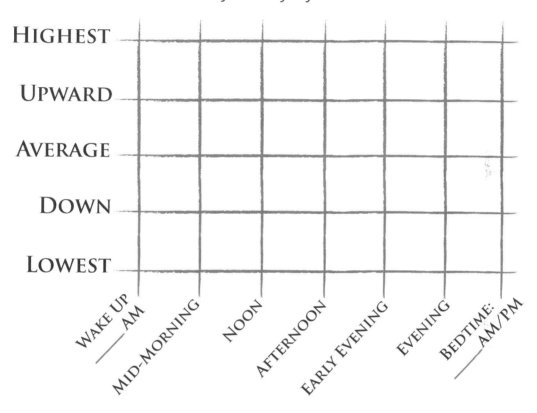

If you're like most people, you have at least one upward spike in the mid-morning, and another spike in the early evening (or later, if you are a teenager or young adult). Why is this important? Because in order to make the best use of your time, you need to do your hardest work when you are most 'up' or alert. A good rule of thumb is:

- ❑ **AM Spike**–Transactional work (math, accounting) and receptive communications (reading, lectures)
- ❑ **PM Spike**–Expressive communications (writing, speaking)

Creating (and Keeping) a Calendar

Okay, so now we have the information we need to create a solid, working calendar—something that actually takes into consideration:

- ❑ What exactly you need to do at the task level (rather than at the generic 'homework' or 'work' level);
- ❑ What your daily routine looks like (meaning, when you have time to do all of this work);
- ❑ What you need to do to have fun (that was on your list, too, remember?) so that we make sure you have time to relax as well; and finally,
- ❑ What your energy level is like throughout the day—because it makes no sense to try to do the majority of your 'thinking' work when you are at your lowest energy level (which is what you are probably doing now, with poor results!).

Now with all of that information, we can create a workable calendar each week that will help you get and stay on top of your 'seven most important things.' The important points to remember about this calendar are:

- ❑ **It does no good if you don't use it**. And so, starting now, each Sunday evening you will need to sit down and plan out your week.
- ❑ **It does no good if you never look at it throughout the week**. Therefore, you will be asked to look at it every morning, both to see what lies ahead and to make sure the work you have allocated time for actually gets done.
- ❑ **You will resist it if you make it rigid**. Things come up, both good and bad, and every calendar or schedule has to change from time to time. That's okay. Make room for the good stuff, deal with the bad stuff, and keep on keepin' on. It's a tool, not a death sentence or a reason to not deal with stuff as it comes up!

Okay, so let's get started. First I'm going to show you what my calendar might look like in a typical week as a sample.

I'm a bit of a night owl and get a 'second wind' around 8 pm, and so I do a fair amount of work in the evening. I can function well in the very early morning if I get up at that time, but I typically crash even harder in the afternoon (which is already the time of my lowest energy level), so I would rather work at night. I do my best thinking/

writing/problem solving in the morning and evening. Afternoons are good 'client time,' because interpersonal interaction for me is easy, and I can easily stay focused on them and our conversation even if I'm not up to doing writing tasks or finances.

I integrate my 'down time' with my cooking and family time, and then go back to work when my daughter is in bed.

	Morning	Midday	Afternoon	Early PM	Late PM
Sunday	Sleep until 9 9-10 make breakfast, relax	Relax!	Relax!	Family dinner, movie, TV or games	10-11 review next week 11 bed
Monday	7-8 school drop off 8:30-10 email, phone calls	10-11 client 11-1 get ready for fair 1-2 client	2-3 client 3-4 client 4-5 client	6-9 Transition fair in San Jose	10-11 TV, relax 11 bed
Tuesday	7-8 school drop off 8:30-9 email, phone calls 9-10 client	10-11 client 11-12 client 12-1 client 1-2 phone calls	2-3 client 3-5 dentist	6-8 dinner, family	9-10 email, reports 10-11 TV, relax 11 bed
Wednesday	7-8 school drop off 8:30-10 email, phone calls	10-11 client 11-1 reports 1-2 client	2-3 reports 3-4 client 4-5 client 5:30-6:30 client	6:30 dinner 7-8 client	10-11 TV, relax 11 bed
Thursday	7-8 school drop off 8:30-10 consult	12:30-1:30 client 11-12 client	2-3 client 3-4 email, phone 4-5 client	6-8 dinner, family	9-10 email, reports 10-11 TV, relax 11 bed

Now, this looks like a pretty crazy schedule because most of my tasks last one hour, and I do have to keep track of each and every one. Imagine if your class schedule or your standing meetings at work changed every day! For most of you, blocking off time for 'School' or 'Production Meeting' on your schedule will suffice, and you would not need to mark down each class, because they are pretty much the same every day. So, your calendar may look like one of these on the following page.

Thursday	7-8	ASB meeting
	8-2:20	SCHOOL
	2:30-3:30	Dojo
	4-5	Math tutor
	5-6	Lab notes
	6-7:30	Dinner, chill
	7:30-9:30	Read for USHAP

Or...

Thursday	7-8	Boot camp
	11-12	Production Meeting
	5:00	Dentist appointment
	10-11	ADHD special ABC

Remember, there is no 'right' way to keep a calendar—it's all about what works for you—what you will really use, and what will actually help you better organize.

Different Media for Calendars

How will you keep your calendar? You essentially have these choices:

- ❑ Paper-based only
- ❑ Electronic only
- ❑ Combination of the two

So far, we've just looked at paper-based calendaring—which is one of the simplest ways to stay organized, and for high school and college students, one that you've probably had experience with. This can be in the form of a school or day planner that you purchase. The pros about these are that they are easy to use. The cons are that you have to carry them everywhere if you want to stay current, and they can be relatively expensive, especially if you purchase one of the name brands such as Day-Timer®, Day Runner®, or FranklinPlanner.

Electronic calendars have become immensely popular over the last two decades. First, they are cheap—most computers have a calendaring system as part of the operating system or as part of another core component such as Microsoft Office. To make access even easier, Google has a free calendaring application you can use—all you need is an internet connection. And, you can invite people to share your calendar, publish it to the web, and automatically sync your electronic calendar with your Smartphone.

An additional benefit of electronic calendars is that you can set events to be repeating (which means you don't have to copy the same thing over and over again) and you can set alarms to remind you of an event. These alarms can be set to go off a day in advance or five minutes in advance—whatever will work best for you.

But what if you're a really strong visual person and you need to 'see' your calendar and hang it on the wall? You can still do that with an electronic calendar—you simply print out your calendar by day, week, month etc. This is especially helpful when you have a crazy schedule such as mine with lots of individual tasks that need to be tracked in a day.

An additional 'visual' appeal of electronic calendars is that you can color code activities, so that school could be blue, sports yellow, family events orange, doctor appointments red, and so forth. This makes it incredibly easy for visual people to quickly scan their calendars and know what's coming up. More on that later.

ThoughtBox: Becoming One with Your Calendar

1. Every Sunday evening, spend some time going over your calendar, and deciding how and when your work for the week is going to get done. This allows your brain to create a 'mental map' of the week, and will help you from feeling constantly bombarded as you 'travel' through the week.

2. Every morning, give yourself at least five minutes to review your calendar, on your cell phone, your laptop, or your day planner. Make it part of your routine, along with morning breakfast or coffee.

3. Spend a few minutes 'walking through' the day. Don't just read the words—spend a bit of time thinking about each event—do you need to prepare, gather materials, make a phone call ahead of time, get gas?

4. Also spend a few minutes going through how you will spend your unscheduled time. Do you have chores or errands to do? Homework? Bills? Grocery shopping? Try to make a mental image of the whole day.

5. Keep your calendar with you! If you need to refer to it throughout the day, that's fine. Let it support you through the day!

Making the Choice

Although I really do believe that there is no one best choice for everyone, I think that most of today's teens and young adults will benefit from using an electronic calendaring system. Even if it might seem like it's too much when you're in school, you will likely need something more sophisticated later in the work world. And, there's no time like the present to get into the habit.

Therefore, I strongly urge all of my clients to set up a Google calendar and to purchase a Smartphone of one sort or another, and then jump through the electronic hoops to set them up to sync. Once it's done, it's simple to keep them synced, and it really will pay off handsomely in the future.

Some *Very* Important Tips on Calendaring

A few things to remember moving forward:

- ❑ When you get your syllabi at school, or a new project at work, immediately **enter all of the important milestones** (papers and quizzes or meetings and completion dates) into your calendar. This way, you don't have to worry about remembering when things are due—it is all safely on your calendar.

- ❑ When setting appointments that will require driving time, either leave enough time between appointments, or actually **block out extra time** for the drive.

- ❑ If you need time to **prepare before a meeting** or an event, block that time off, too, on your calendar. Don't get caught in the mad-dash rush to find everything last minute.

- ❑ Whether your calendar is paper-based or electronic, set up and **use a color coding system** for different tasks (red for urgent, blue for business, orange for kids, purple for personal; or, red for Chemistry, blue for Bio, and so forth). This makes your calendar much easier to read.

- ❑ If you are using an electronic calendar, **set alarms to remind you** of upcoming appointments. Choose the reminder time carefully—if you have to drive somewhere and set the alarm to go off 5 minutes before the appointment, you've missed the appointment. Set it for 30 minutes (or more) ahead of the appointment.

- ❑ Be careful when you sync your cell phone to your electronic calendar so that you don't accidentally delete appointments on one or the other. **Create a backup file** of your desktop calendar, and then play around with the settings to see how they work. If you lose your calendar in the process, just use the copy you have saved.

❑ When necessary, add additional information onto your calendar such as **contact name and phone number** (in case you're running late) and address if it's an offsite appointment. This will save you last-minute scurrying to find the info you need, especially if you are running late.

Other Useful Time Management Tools

Although using a calendar may be the most important time management tool you'll use, there are other ways to keep yourself on time and on schedule. What other tools can you use to keep yourself together?

Task Lists

Yes, the world can be divided into those who make lists and those who don't, and while I don't think that everyone needs to make lists for everything they do, task lists do come in handy, especially during a crunch time when there is lots to do and little time to do it. Task lists are also very handy for things that need to be done but don't have to be done at a specific time, like calling to make an appointment with your dentist, or remembering to order a book.

Whether you use Post-It notes, a sheet of paper or the Task List in your Smartphones, task lists are a great place to keep track of all those 'little things' that never get done or all those items you keep forgetting to pick up at the grocery store. Plus, there is great satisfaction in checking items off lists as completed—some people will even add things to their task lists that they have already done, just to inspire them to keep on going!

Visual Cues

Another useful—and very low tech—way of staying organized is to use a chalkboard or whiteboard to track important items you need to do. This is especially useful when it's 'crunch time' and you have a lot of things that need to get done in a short amount of time. This strategy is especially useful for those who are visual thinkers—seeing it visually helps you to map out your life in a spatial, tangible way.

Also, don't forget about plain old Post-It® notes. A neon pink reminder by the door to take a book back to school may be just the ticket to help remind you to perform this task. However, if you try to use the Post-It® method for ongoing events, like taking out the trash every Friday, over time you will stop 'seeing' the note, and will forget again—better to put repeating events on your calendar where you have to actually respond to the reminder each time. Another way to use Post-Its® is on calendars—one Post-It® for each task. This allows you to move the Post-It from day to day if your schedule is changeable.

ThoughtBox: Why We Write Things Down

One of the things I have learned is that the brain is a very powerful database—if we learn how to use it properly.

Our brains naturally want to sort and store information. Whether or not we know it, our brains are making millions of 'decisions' every day about what information to retain and what to throw out, and much of this processing is unconscious.[1] However, when bombarded by so much information every day, your brain cannot always retain and recall what you want it to. This is where writing things down helps, especially for those who are 'visuals' or who have difficulty with auditory processing.

Writing things down creates a picture of sorts, and is a form of *intentionally encoding*[2] a thought for later recall. This may be why students state that taking notes in class helps them learn the material, even if they never look at those notes again.[3] The act of the note taking itself seems to help recall even if you don't actually try to memorize the material.

So, write things down. Re-read what you have written, or better yet—read your list or notes out loud—which uses kinesthetic (writing), visual (reading), and auditory (speaking) senses. See if using this multi-modal strategy helps your brain hang on to the information you want it to remember!

1   C. Koch, N. Tsuchiya (2006). Attention and consciousness: two distinct brain processes. *Trends in Cognitive Sciences*, 11 (1), pp. 16-22.
2   C. Williams (2010). Incidental and intentional visual memory: What memories are and are not affected by encoding tasks? *Visual Cognition*, 18 (9), pp. 1348-1367.
3   V. Kalnikaite and S. Whittaker (2007). Does taking notes help you remember better? *Exploring How Note Taking Relates to Memory*. Presented September 4, 2007, at the British HCI conference, Lancaster, UK.

Auditory Cues

Some folks prefer auditory cues over visual ones, and that's fine. Your reminders on your cell phones and desktop computers are auditory as well as visual, but there are other cues you can use.

One of the simplest is to call yourself and leave a message on your land line or cell phone. This is a very simple way to remind yourself to do something when you are at another location, such as 'look for the book I borrowed from John.' The key here is that when you listen to the message, you must actually go do that task right then and there, or it will be forgotten again!

Other auditory cues are alarm clocks and timers. Although we use alarm clocks to wake up in the morning, we can also use them throughout the day to remind us to take medication, make a phone call, etc. We can also use timers in much of the same way— remember when to take dinner out of the oven, when to leave for an appointment, to time how long you are playing on the computer. All of these work!

Where Does the Time Go?

If you are like most of us, there are times when you simply lose track of time and you find yourself caught in a bind and rushing to finish something. If this happens only every so often, it's not a problem. But, if you find yourself over and over again unable to finish your work, even with all of these time management skills in place, you may need to dig a little deeper to see what is keeping you from success.

Overactive Response Systems

Some of us get caught up in distractions and interruptions—we seem incapable of focusing on the task at hand for all the things going on around us. But, some of these things can and should be avoided—we just need to tell ourselves that we do not need to attend to the interruption, and can safely ignore it.

One way that we get caught up in distractions is by an 'overactive' limbic system. We'll talk about sensory challenges a bit later, but right now know that we are built to respond to sensory input—and for the most part, that's a good thing—if we smell something burning, our brain tells us to go look and see if there is danger. If we hear our alarm clock go off in the morning, our brain tells us to wake up. If we see someone in distress, our brain tells us to offer help. This is our limbic system at work—our limbic system is the complex system in our brains that takes in sensory input and instructs the body how to respond. Hear a bell? Turn and look. See something flying toward your face? Flinch and hold your hand up.

But, sometimes our brains are good at fooling us into believing that we should respond to all sensory input, even though that input that has no real meaning to us. This is where we get in trouble—we are no longer selective about the stimuli we respond to, but instead respond to all of it equally, because our 'filters' aren't working as well as they should. Take this little test to see how you fare:

1.	I turn to see who it is whenever the door opens, even when I'm somewhere public like school, a restaurant or work.	❏ T	❏ F
2.	I have a hard time ignoring my cell phone or an IM chime and have to see who it is, even if I'm studying or reading.	❏ T	❏ F
3.	I have to read every email immediately as it comes in, or I'm uncomfortable.	❏ T	❏ F
4.	If I feel a cool breeze, I have to get up to close the window or to put on a sweater right away.	❏ T	❏ F
5.	I have a hard time not looking at something my classmate has in his or her hands.	❏ T	❏ F
6.	If my stomach growls, I immediately get up to get something to eat.	❏ T	❏ F

If you answered True to more than two, then you may be an 'over-responder,' and allow sensory stimulation to interfere with your focus on the task at hand. The first step to stop over-responding is to be aware that you are doing it. See if you can keep track of how many times for the rest of the day (or tomorrow, if it's late) you find yourself interrupted by the world around you when you are trying to focus.

You'll likely find that when you are in your upper swings on your daily biorhythms, you are less distractible. And the opposite is true, as well–when you're tired and cranky, you're far more likely to have difficulty with focus.

All of us can get better at focusing, and with a little work, you can teach yourself to not respond to every distraction. On the next page, we have another test to demonstrate how our brains can fool us. Can you identify the most rational response?

Sensory Input/Thoughts	Possible Explanations
The dog is barking	The dog is miserable, and I must let him in at once before he perishes from grief.
	The dog is barking at a cat and is fine.
	The dog is barking at a friend who is stopping by unannounced—I have to check who it is!
The phone is ringing	It's someone calling to tell me I just won a million dollars! Yay!
	It's probably someone for my mom so I'll let the answering machine get it.
	It might be someone trying to call 911, and they misdialed, and I need to help them—it's life or death!
I am hungry	I am ravenous and I need to make a batch of brownies from scratch right now or I will die.
	I will not be able to do anything else until I get food into my stomach, so I'll just walk two miles each way to 7-11 and get a quick bite to eat.
	Dinner is in 20 minutes, so I'll just wait. My girlfriend gets mad if I eat a snack right before dinner anyway.

How do you think you did? Clearly, these are a bit over the top, but let's go over them. A dog barking at a cat is probably okay, unless the dog or the cat sounds like it's in pain. If the phone rings, let the answering machine get it, unless you are actually expecting a call. And if you're hungry, think about when the next meal is. I know from my own experience that there's nothing that frustrates the family cook (mom or dad) more than a kid or spouse who isn't hungry for dinner prepared because they just had a boatload of snacks! Can you wait until dinner? Or maybe a small snack will tide you over. In the meantime, get back to work!

Generic Time Wasters

When I was a junior and senior in college, you could always tell when finals were closing in, because my house was absolutely spotless. My generic time waster was cleaning the house. While housecleaning is generally not thought of as a waste of time, it was the way I would distract myself from doing what I really needed to be doing—writing papers.

We can find all sorts of ways to distract ourselves—it isn't hard. And frequently we distract ourselves with things that *should* be done, just not right now! Or, we find ourselves caught up in something that is perfectly fine to do some of the time (such as gaming, texting, chatting, surfing the internet) but sucks us in to the point where we don't get the things done we want to get done.

What are your generic time wasters? Things that you 'indulge' in a little too much, and you know get in the way of doing the things you want to accomplish? List them here:

My Time Wasters	Hours a Week
1	
2	
3	
4	
5	
6	
7	
8	
9	
10	
11	
12	
Total	

Just being aware of where your time goes can help you maintain better control of what you are doing, and for how long. No one expects you to give up all of your guilty pleasures, just to find balance.

Computer and Internet Use

Yep, this gets its own section. Why? Because computer and internet use can become a huge problem. So much so, that a new term has been coined when referring to it—Problematic Internet Usage or PIU—and it is recognized as a true type of addiction. Now, this isn't to say that the computer is dangerous or that casually surfing the 'Net while eating your lunch is a problem.

But, like with most things, if you spend too much time engaging in this activity, you will be missing out on a lot of other activities that are perhaps more important or fulfilling. This is when use crosses into abuse—when you use it to avoid other activities. And, abuse crosses over into true addiction when you feel compelled to get on the internet, and actually feel uncomfortable if you can't get your electronic fix. You have to do it.

Gaming and surfing the internet may seem harmless, and they are for the most part. However, if you are avoiding things you should be doing, falling behind in class or work, not interacting with friends or family as much as you used to, then you may need help to break the habit and get back to the real world.

Part of this is biochemical, which reinforces the habit—you get a hit of 'happy hormones' (dopamine, serotonin, etc.) when you read a text message, level up in a game, or post on Reddit. You become the little lab rat sucking on this hormonal solution, addicted to the high. This is becoming such a common problem that some therapists are specializing in helping people break the habit. You are not alone, and if this is a problem, seek help from a qualified mental health professional.

The Truth about Procrastination

Many people who have difficulty managing their time are accused of being lazy or procrastinating. So what is procrastination and how is it different from wasting time? Well, the two are somewhat related—people procrastinate by using time wasters, but they can also procrastinate by doing things they should be doing, just not right now (like cleaning your house!).

However, some people prefer having the pressure of the impending deadline in order to perform—and feel that the adrenaline rush of 'ohmigod, I gotta get crackin!' is actually motivating to them to do their best work.[1] However, there is certainly a fine line between waiting until you are good and ready to do the work, and waiting too long and not being able to perform at your best. Plus, remember Murphy's Law—if something can go wrong, it will.

My son, who is a veteran procrastinator, found this out when he went to print out his paper due that morning at 8 AM—only to find out that the toner cartridge was empty. He was not met with great sympathy when he woke me up to tell me this at 3 AM. If you really feel you need the pressure, that's okay—but start at the next-to-last-minute

---

1   Olafson, L., Schraw, G., Wadkins, T. (2007). Doing the things we do: A grounded theory of academic procrastination. *Journal of Educational Psychology*, Vol 99, No. 1, (12-25).

rather than the actual last minute. And if you can do some of the work early on, that will help as well. We'll talk later on about why starting early matters so that we can use our ability to unconsciously process information to more easily do our work.

ADHD, Sensory, Depressive, and Anxiety Challenges—Which Affect Us All!

Beyond the issues that we have discussed here, some people have an even more difficult time staying focused and using their time 'wisely.' All of the techniques in this chapter will help, but individuals with specific challenges may need a bit more help in managing time. **Even if you don't have one of these challenges, read through for ideas on how to manage when you are really struggling with time management**.

ADHD

It shouldn't be surprising that those individuals who have Attention Deficit, Hyperactivity Disorder (also known as Attention Deficit) often have a very difficult time staying on task and not wandering off mentally to join the party in their head—distractibility is almost always part of the diagnosis. A few things that may help include:

- ❑ Frequent breaks with physical activity
- ❑ Listening to music at a very low level
- ❑ Using a fidget or doodle while thinking or reading
- ❑ Sucking on a sour candy
- ❑ Drinking cold water

Some people with ADHD have had good luck with neurofeedback or biofeedback treatment, Interactive Metronome, or cognitive retraining such as a CogMed. You can find more information about each of these on the internet (just remember to get off!). In many cases, individuals with ADHD may also benefit from one of the medications used to increase focus.

Sensory Processing Disorder

Sensory Processing Disorder, or SPD, causes the brain to either overreact or underreact to stimuli in the environment. Sometimes the individual will be very sensitive to certain sounds or to loud noises. Other times, the person may dislike the way things feel, and may be unable to sit still in a chair for very long. In these cases, usually the best strategy is to either screen the stimuli, such as listening to low level music, pink or white noise (sounds at different hertz levels—see www.simplynoise.com), wrapping up in a tight blanket, fingering a specific texture, or diffusing the air with a specific aroma that the individual prefers.

While this all may seem silly to those who do not have SPD, please be aware that individuals with SPD really can suffer from their overactive senses. Individuals with hyperactive sensory challenges typically fall into a cycle where the undesirable stimuli kicks off their limbic system, releasing adrenaline into their system which raises anxiety to such a level that the person cannot focus until the anxiety—and the attendant causes—are dealt with.

In fact, many individuals who are diagnosed with ADHD may have underlying sensory issues that are not properly diagnosed or treated, confounding clinicians, parents, and the individual. Again, there is a great deal of information about SPD on the internet, along with ideas for treatment.

Depression

We know that a common cause for distractibility is depression (indeed, it is one of the possible criteria for diagnosis),[2] and those with long-term depression can find it very difficult to accomplish even the barest of necessary tasks. Depression is caused by an imbalance in our brain chemistry, which in turn seems to interrupt our ability to focus for any length of time. If depression is the (or one of the) culprits, the depression must be treated therapeutically before the individual can function well.

Anxiety

Anxiety is another common cause of distractibility.[3] Like depression, the brain chemistry is interrupted, which in turn makes it very difficult to focus. And like depression, those with anxiety will find it very difficult to master time management until they treat the underlying anxiety.

2   American Psychiatric Association. (2013). Diagnostic and statistical manual of mental disorders (5th ed.). Arlington, VA: American Psychiatric Publishing. pp. 155-188.

3   Ibid. pp. 189-233.

ThoughtBox: Your Brain as a Filter

Our brains act like an aperture on a camera, opening and closing to let in sensory information. The wider the aperture, or filter, is opened, the more information, and distraction, that gets in. The smaller the aperture is closed, the less sensory data gets in, which can cause us to be inattentive and feel sluggish. How can you increase or decrease sensory input in your environment to get to your 'just right' state?

In Defense of Taking (Many Short) Breaks

I have heard from many of my clients that one of the things they hate more than anything is being reminded to 'get back to work' by their parents, spouses, bosses, or other well-meaning, but somewhat-misguided, individuals.

Let's be clear—it is not helpful to interrupt someone who is trying to work, just like it makes no sense to wake up a patient to give them a sleeping pill. And, the stress inflicted by the demand 'get back to work' only makes the 'getting' harder.

Being able to identify when you are no longer productive and take appropriate remedial steps takes some time to master, but it's an important skill for everyone to do, because we do indeed all get stuck from time to time.

Just like it's a bad idea to stay in bed if you can't sleep, it's a bad idea to keep sitting at the desk (or table, or whatever) if you can't work. It only increases anxiety and reinforces the negativity you feel while sitting there doing 'nothing.' Instead, set a kitchen timer and set it for 10 minutes. When the timer goes off, do one of these things for 5-10 minutes:

- ❑ Get up and either ride a bike or 'power walk' for five minutes, then return to your work
- ❑ Stretch or do a little yoga
- ❑ Do jumping jacks or other aerobic exercise
- ❑ Sing or play a musical instrument
- ❑ Eat a piece of fruit or a protein-rich snack (like nuts or a hard-boiled egg)
- ❑ Use sensory stimulants such as sour candy, cold water, fidgets, music, soothing sounds, or pink or white noise (www.simplynoise.com)

Note that the best things to do to regain your focus and energy is to get up and move—deeper breathing reoxygenates the blood, which in turn pumps more oxygen into your brain, thus making you more alert. Plus, the physical exercise 'burns off' adrenaline and cortisol (reducing anxiety and jittery-ness), and the added endorphins from doing something pleasurable like singing or stretching add to your 'happy load' so you can regain focus more easily. Simple biochemistry!

Things you *must avoid* on your breaks, as they will only suck you in, and discourage you from getting back to work:

❏ The Internet (including chat, texting, IMing, reading email)
❏ TV
❏ Gaming

Over time, try increasing the length of time you can stay focused by setting a timer for 10, then 15, and eventually up to 30 minutes. However, if you find yourself wandering, no matter how long you have been working, get up and take a break and try again. If after three attempts you just can't get into the focus groove, take a break for an hour or longer and try later. You can't make yourself focus, and it's better to take a break and try to identify what is going on in your brain that is hindering your progress.

As an aside, what to do if you're a parent or a boss, and can see that your kid or worker is off track, lost in the clouds, or otherwise not getting any work done? First, make sure that they are not just thinking—if so, let them be. If they really are in the weeds, don't admonish. It won't work. Instead, tell them to get up and take a break. Help them learn how to manage his/her attentional state.

Your Action Plan

This chapter has covered a lot of ground about time management, and we'll refer back to these concepts in later chapters. But hopefully you have learned a little bit about how you work, what's important to you, how you get off track, and how to get back on track. At this point, you have enough information to redo a few of the exercises we did at the beginning of the chapter. And I just bet you might have a few changes!

Identifying What's Important

Write down your priorities again. They may be the same as before, or they may be different. What seven things are the most important to you?

My Seven Important Things	Hours Spent	Hours Needed
1		
2		
3		
4		
5		
6 Downtime		
7 Social life		
Totals Per Week:		

And as before, estimate how many hours you spend on each priority and how much time is actually needed.

Putting It Together

On the next few pages, you will find space to write down what you have learned about yourself in terms of your Time Management Profile—this will help you make better use of your time moving forward.

Additionally, here are some reminders about what we covered, and your action plan on how to make this work for you:

1. **Weekly Strategy Session**—On your cell phone, set a repeating alarm for a convenient time on Sunday afternoon or evening for 30 minutes to go over your calendar for the coming week. If you need to take time to break tasks down, set aside time to work on planning, make sure you add that time in as well.

2. **Daily Check-ins**—Again, on your cell phone, set a repeating alarm for each work or school day in the morning for a five-minute check-in to go over your calendar for the day. Really read the calendar entries, walk through what you need to do, what you need to have ready, how long it will take to get to an appointment, and so forth.

3. **Notice and Note Distractions**—Keep a running list on what things, people, activities distract you the most. Think about ways you can change up your environment to keep yourself distraction-free.

4. **Focus on the Focus**—When you are really 'in the flow,' stop to think about why—what is going on in your environment (or not going on) that really helps you get the work done? Finding out what works for you, so that you can replicate it later, is part of discovering your own inner CEO.

5. **Don't Go It Alone**—If you are trying to learn these new skills alone, it may be hard to stay on task. Find a buddy to do this work with, and plan on holding each other accountable for their ability to keep on top of their time management skills.

Your Time Management Profile

Now that you've learned the key points of time management, take the time to go back through this chapter, and make some notes about what your time management profile is:

My Best Times:	
To read difficult text	
To do my standard work or homework	
To do difficult problem-solving	
To do my writing	
To do emails, texts, return phone calls	
During these times of days, my biggest distractions are:	
AM	
Midday	
Afternoon	
Evening	
Ways I can regain focus:	
AM	
Midday	
Afternoon	
Evening	
Times I am most likely to need a break:	

How I Am Distracted

HOW I FOCUS

Space Management

It may sound a bit odd to talk about physical environment in the context of organization, but there is a very good reason why our environment must be conducive to work and organization—if our personal or work space is chaotic, noisy, cluttered, most of us feel that much more easily distracted and stressed.[1] Additionally, when we are stressed, under deadline, and already feeling a bit out of control, having a cluttered environment can send us over the edge. We search for tools we need and cannot find them. We try to focus on the work on our computer, and the phone is ringing and people are talking. We look around the room and see 500 things we need to take care of. No wonder we cannot get anything done!

What does YOUR work environment look like (your dorm, your office, your kitchen table)? Take a few minutes to describe it, and make sure you describe noise, clutter, and other environmental factors:

_____

_____

_____

_____

_____

_____

_____

_____

---

1   http://www.closetsdaily.com/closet-news/closets-industry-news/rubbermaid_survey_shows_clutter_leads_to_stress_129230503.html, accessed February 19, 2012.

THE CEO OF SELF

Now, take a few minutes to close your eyes, and imagine what this space would look like if you could make it any way you wanted it to be. Make sure to include ALL the details you want—lighting, music or background noise, chair, desk, whatever—describe it all. If it helps, draw the ideal work space below as well.

_____

_____

_____

_____

_____

_____

MY WORKSPACE

What is different between the two? One is the reality and the other is the desired outcome. You may not be able to do everything (a new plasma TV may not be in the budget, and probably won't help you focus), but certainly there are some things you can do to make your environment more conducive to the work you want to do. Let's get started.

A Place for Everything...

And everything in its place...although this is a trite saying, it is the cornerstone for organization. Imagine if you will—there was no organization at all in your home. Your toothbrush is in the garage. The frying pan is under the bed. Your shoes are on the top shelf in the kitchen cupboard. Your money is in a bathroom drawer. Your ATM card is under the flowerpot. Your keys are in the dishwasher.

Sounds crazy, right? How would you ever find things? You couldn't.

Our brains like structure. They like organization. They like to sort things. Now, the extent to which our brains like to sort things varies greatly from person to person, but the point is—we all have a natural inclination to sort. Big to small. Most to least. Like to like. Even if the only organization we really have is by room (I'm pretty sure all of my underwear belongs in my bedroom, and the blender belongs in the kitchen), that is sorting and sorting creates structure. We have created consistent 'buckets' to store stuff in so that we can more easily retrieve stuff when we need it.

Our brains work in the same way, so why not make it easy on ourselves, and store information logically so it can recall that information for us later when we need it? It's the same logic—it doesn't matter whether we are asking our brains to remember to buy butter at the store, or asking it to remember where we put our keys. If we are consistent in giving our brains enough input so that it can retrieve that info later, we are in much better shape. Here are some very simple tips to get you started.

Your Most-Lost Items

Most of us have at least one item we are forever losing or misplacing. Keys, cell phones, and wallets are among the top faves for losing, but yours might be different. Here's the trick: always put them in the same place every day, and you will always be able to find them. It's so simple, and yet so many of us fail to do this.

For women who carry purses, and guys (and women) who use backpacks, this is simple—keep everything in your backpack. After you unlock the door, put the keys back in your backpack. After you purchase a song on iTunes, put the credit card back into your wallet and the wallet back into your backpack. When your phone is done charging, put it back into your backpack. Where do these things go? Into your backpack!

Okay, okay, not everything will fit into your backpack. Or, maybe you don't carry one.

That's fine. Instead, you need to pick one place where you will keep these items. A bowl on the kitchen counter. A small box in the entryway. The left-hand corner on your dresser. As designers of computer software know, *where* doesn't matter as much as consistency.[2] You need to religiously keep all of your stuff together in one place so that when you are packing up to leave the house you have one stop to gather your stuff, instead of hunting around the house for the things you need. Here are some of the places I keep things, to give you an idea:

❑ My office key is on a stretchy band that goes around my wrist while I'm at work, and hangs on the rearview mirror in my car when I'm not. I take the key off my wrist and hang it up before I back out of my parking space at work every single day. I keep it with me all day because I need to have it with me to open the rest room door (too many times have I walked down the hall only to remember I don't have the key!).

❑ The front right corner of the chest of drawers in the front hall at home is where I keep things that need to be taken to work—packages to be mailed, art supplies, etc. I have to walk by that chest of drawers each morning on my way to the car. If it fits in my computer bag and needs to be taken to work, I simply put it in my computer bag. I never leave for work without my laptop!

❑ The front right corner of the main desk at my office for things going home—articles to read, empty lunch containers, etc. If I put it there, I will pick it up on the way out. If I leave it somewhere else, it will never get home.

❑ The kitchen desk is where I keep all of my chargers—phones, Bluetooth, the dog's anti-barking collar, all go there. The exception to this is my Kindle Fire. I keep that by my bedside, wrapped around the bedpost, so it is handy when I'm playing, because I always use my Kindle in bed.

List your most frequently lost (or forgotten) items and describe where you keep them—or where you are going to start keeping them:

Cell phone	
Wallet	
Keys	
Purse/Backpack	

---

2   Tan, D., Stefanucci, J., Proffitt, D. and Pausch, R. (2001). The infocockpit: Providing location and place to aid human memory. Proceedings of the 2001 *Workshop on Perceptive User Interfaces*. Published by ACM, New York, NY, 2001. Pp. 1-4.

Handiness Items

Another great way to 'sort' things is to keep them where they are most handy or easy to access. Using the example above, I keep my Kindle charger by my bed, not in the kitchen with my other charges. The reason being that I use my Kindle almost exclusively in bed, and I want it (and the charger) handy if I'm snuggled into bed and need to play Scrabble™ to unwind before sleep.

You probably have lots of 'stored for handiness' items in your home already. The toilet paper is not in the trunk of your car (for long, anyway). The cereal is not in the garden. You keep these things near to where you will use them so that you're not running all over the house when you need something. You want them to be handy.

So, mentally walk through your home or office, and name a few things that are kept where they are just for 'handiness':

What?	Where?

Frequently-Used Items

Like 'handy' items, some items are kept where they are because they are used frequently. For example, in the kitchen, we tend to keep the things we use the most stored between our waist and our eyes, because they are in view and easy to reach.

Generally speaking, you want to keep your most frequently used items easily accessible so you're not on your hands and knees rooting around in the cupboards every day. (Next time you're at the supermarket, check out what is on the top and bottom shelves—stuff that is either unusual (top) or cheap (bottom)—the things they expect or want you to buy are in the middle!)

Infrequently-Used Items

And...the reverse is true as well. If you don't use something frequently, it can safely be stashed somewhere that requires a little getting-to to retrieve. Save your 'easily accessible' spots for things you use frequently, and keep Aunt Mildred's purple crocheted tea cozy in the very bottom drawer under the Halloween towels. Some things are meant to be forgotten!

List a few locations where you store 'use frequently' items, and a few locations where you store 'use infrequently' items:

What?	Where?

'Like with Like' Items

Like a big Dewey Decimal system in the library, we frequently keep things in our homes (offices, lockers, backpacks) based on similarity—all the biographies in one place, picture books in another, and so forth. And indeed, some people keep all of their books in one room, sorted by type, DVDs in another room sorted by title, and so forth. If we are looking for a Blu-Ray, we know exactly where to look. Another thing you can keep together is your loose change—get a big jar or bottle and put all of your coins in it, and then sort it later. You will be amazed how much money piles up after several months!

This *like with like* system is so natural that many of our software programs sort things for us—iTunes for example can sort all of your music by genre. *Like with like.* That way, you won't have to endure the transition from Bohemian Rhapsody to The Hamster Dance.

If you have ever collected something like rocks, fossils, stamps, plastic horses, then you have kept like things with like. In fact, that's what a collection is—a group of objects that are similar in one or more ways.

What types of collections (DVDs, books, games) do you have and where do you keep them?

What?	Where?

ThoughtBox: What to Do If You Can't Remember to 'Put it Away'

Okay, you say, you understand why it's important to have one place to put things, but you simply forget and drop your phone or keys without thinking and then can't find them. The key here is 'without thinking,' right?

I bought a new purse a few months ago, and instead of putting my keys in the outside pocket where I could quickly retrieve them, I kept dropping them into the main compartment, which meant that I would spend frustrating minutes trying to retrieve them from amidst the rest of the stuff I keep in there. Aha! I was doing it, too!

So, I sat down with my purse and consciously put my keys in the outside pocket, reminding myself why I was doing this. I repeated this several times—"I am putting my keys in the outside pocket so that I can easily find them." I took them out, and did it again, and again.

Guess where my keys are right now, and have been each day since I did this? Be mindful. Practice. Tell your brain why you are doing this act so that it can work with you, instead of against you. If you slip up, just repeat the exercise, and remind your brain (really, your conscious mind) why you are doing this.

Reminder Items

This is another category of sorting—keeping things where we will see them, trip over them, hear them, and the like—in fact, their location may be part of their purpose.

Alarm clocks fall into this category. They do no good in waking us up in the morning if we can't hear them. So, they typically go by our bed. (And a note, here—if you are one of the many who simply rolls over and turns off the alarm without actually waking up, turn the alarm to the most annoying sound it makes, and move the alarm clock across the room so that you have to get out of bed to turn it off. And do not go back to bed!)

Answering machines (which will soon be a thing of the past) are another reminder item. If we don't see them blinking at us, we won't know there are messages on it. For that reason, we typically put them in a room that we frequent, such as the kitchen, so that we will see that someone has called.

Other ways we 'organize' our living spaces to remind us to do things include putting the garbage or recycling by the door, tape memos to our doors, and so forth. How have you 'organized' your space to help you remember things?

What?	Where?

Keepin' It Simple

A few years back, I read an article in a magazine describing how we Americans are so driven to have everything, that much of what we own is redundant or overly specialized, and that we were drowning in our stuff. Case in point—why would anyone ever buy (and store) a pop-up hotdog warmer when we have microwaves, stoves, ovens, and BBQ grills? I liked this concept so much, that I began to look through my kitchen. Did I need to own a mortar and pestle and a spice grinder and a coffee grinder and a food processor and a blender and a hand held mixer and a stationary mixer and a set of three French whisks?

Um, probably not, but I do indeed own all of these things.

The time to think about whether or not you need more stuff is when you have the phone in one hand and the credit card in the other. Or, when you're surfing the 'Net. Or, standing in line at the store. Ask yourself—do I have something else already that will do the same job just as well? If so, do you really need to spend your money, clutter your life, and create a larger carbon footprint by buying more stuff? Will it genuinely make your life easier, make you happier, or in any way noticeably improve your life?

If not, put it down and walk away. Be free. Liberate yourself from stuff!

What ways can you simplify your life? What do you have (or want) that you don't need and can safely—and maybe even happily—do without?

_____

_____

_____

_____

_____

_____

Undoing Overwhelm—Breakin' It Down

If you're like most folks, picking up and cleaning the house is probably not at the top of your list of things to do when you have a few extra minutes. And, like many people, you probably face a pretty big mess once in a while—big enough so that it can be intimidating and overwhelming, and you may give up before you even start.

But, cleaning does not have to be that way. You don't have to spend hours a week cleaning your house, and you don't have to be a neat freak to have a tidy home! Here are a few methods that really work.

15-Minute Pickup

This is my favorite, fast, effective method of getting my living space back into reasonable condition. It's simple, and can even be more fun if you do it with family members or roommates.

1. Select one of your favorite songs with a really fast beat. Turn the volume up loud enough so that you can hear it throughout your living space, but not so loud as to offend the neighbors (Note: this is a daytime activity!).

2. Starting in one room, scan and pick up everything that goes in your bedroom. Run to your bedroom, and throw everything in your arms on the bed.

3. Now, in the bedroom, scan and pick up everything that goes in the kitchen and/or bathroom.

4. Run first to the bathroom, and drop off bathroom items there.

5. Next, run to the kitchen, and drop off kitchen items there. Scan the kitchen for items that belong elsewhere in the house. Pick them up, and take them where they belong—just drop them off for now.

6. Go back to the room where you started (probably the living room or family room) and scan the room for all items that go in the kitchen.

7. Drop kitchen stuff off in the kitchen.

Your living space is now picked up (or darn close)! Now, as time permits, go back to each room and simply put the things away that you returned to their proper room. If you don't have time to do it right now, make a pact with yourself that the next time you are in that room, you will take the time to put things away. If you do this once or twice a week, your living space will be much more orderly, and will not feel overwhelming.

15-Minute Cleanups

Once the house is picked up, you can go on to cleaning it if you have another 15 minutes and some helpers. If you are doing this work solo, pick two tasks to do, and then do another task or two tomorrow. These cleaning chores are much easier to do after you have picked up everything and moved them to their appropriate rooms, and if you do the same task in each room, one by one, you won't get bogged down in one place.

Trash/Recycling

1. Scan the kitchen for trash, and place it all in the garbage

2. Take the garbage bag to the living/family room. Scan for garbage, pick it up, go to the bedroom(s).

3. Scan for garbage, pick it up, take the trash out

4. Repeat for recycling

Dishes/Kitchen

1. Go back to the kitchen and load the dishes in the dishwasher

2. Wash all other items

3. Wipe down counters

4. Damp mop floor with a Swiffer® or other spray mop with disposable sheets

Bedroom

1. Put away all stuff on your bed from the 15-minute pickup

2. Pick up all dirty laundry and put it in the hamper

3. Hang up all other clothes

4. Put shoes away

5. Stack books, CDs, games, etc.

Bathroom

1. Put away all the items from the 15-minute pickup

2. Spray shower/tub and sink with bathroom cleaning spray and let sit

3. Spray toilet cleaner into toilet and let sit

4. Wipe off mirrors

5. Wipe out sink

6. Brush toilet

7. Spray off shower/tub

8. Wipe down counters

9. Damp mop floor with Swiffer® or other spray mop with disposable sheets

Living Areas

1. Put away all the items from the 15-minute pickup

2. Sort through newspapers and magazines, and throw out old stuff

3. Put away gaming stuff, toys, books

4. Wipe or dust off coffee and end tables

5. Damp mop floor with Swiffer® or other spray mop with disposable sheets and/or

6. Vacuum carpet

Now, if you and your family or roommates do these two 15-minute exercises every week, your house will never get overwhelming, and you can literally get it all done in 30-60 minutes a week, and have a lovely place to live—and be able to find everything! Wow!

The Archeological Dig

Okay. So, you didn't keep up on the housework. You haven't done your little routines to keep the place picked up. And now—full-on chaos. If you're lucky, there's at least a path from the door to the bed, and there may be one clean glass left in the cupboard. But that's about it.

It may be so bad, that you don't even want to go home. Or you have even considered calling the health department on yourself just so that someone else would come in and clean it up. Even if it means going to packrat jail while they cleaned it for you. It would be worth it, right?

Well, no. And barring any live critters living under the dirty clothes, it probably isn't all that bad. But, it will require a different tactic. We call this the Archeological Dig, where you work on three square feet at a time.

You'll need:

1. A garbage can

2. A bucket for dirty dishes

3. A hamper for dirty clothes

4. Another basket to put stuff in to sort later

5. A shopping bag to put important papers in to sort later

Starting in one corner of one room, pick up items and decide—do I need it or want it anymore? If not, throw it away. If so, put it in the appropriate receptacle. Keep going, one item at a time, until one of your buckets, baskets or bags is filled. Take a break, put the dishes in the dishwasher, take the laundry to the washing machine, empty the garbage. Then go back, and do it again. You'd be surprised at how quickly this will go, and pretty soon you will have at least sorted everything into their appropriate piles.

When you've finished one room, run the dishes, wash the clothes, empty the trash, and call it a day. Next time you sit down to watch TV or a movie, sort through the items in the important paper bag or the basket of stuff. More on this in the *Painless Multitasking* section in a few pages.

Once you have picked up one or more rooms, go back and actually clean the room—vacuum, dust, and sponge-clean waterproof surfaces. If the room is really clean, you will have more impetus to keep it clean by using the 15-minute routines.

Spring (and Summer, Fall, Winter) Cleaning

Even if you keep your house pretty picked up and pretty clean, over time it will get gross—dust bunnies accumulate in the corners, grease on the walls, streaks on the windows. At this point, you have a couple of choices:

❑ Hire someone to come in and 'deep clean' the place

❑ Do a thorough cleaning in one room once or twice a year (more if you can)

❑ Ignore it and give up your cleaning deposit when you move out, and don't plan on having anyone of the opposite sex (or same sex, if applicable) over for a romantic evening. If you're a parent, don't expect your kids to want to bring their friends home to play, which could be a benefit, I suppose!

Now, younger folk, and men in general, seem to have what I call a higher 'scuzz factor,' meaning that dirt, grime, and mess don't bother them as much as others, particularly mothers (and certainly, mothers-in-law). So, maybe it doesn't bug you much. But, it really can become gross over time, and remember that you can keep it clean, or make it clean, if you choose. Start with the previous sections, pick up, do the easier stuff, and then do the deep stuff. Pretty soon, you'll have a lovely place to live—all the time.

The Pen Cup Exercise

No matter where you live, and no matter how clean you keep things, stuff accumulates. It just does. Drawers get cluttered. Papers pile up. Ripped clothes stay in the closet for years. Dried up pens stay in the pencil cup by the phone.

You know this one, right? You pick a pen up and try to write with it. It doesn't work. You put it back in the cup, and try another one. It doesn't work. You put it back, and take another one until you finally find one that works. What is up with *that*? Mindlessness, and we all do it.

So how about trying this? If you're on the phone yakking with a friend, just dump all of the pens out on the table, grab a piece of scratch paper, and test them one by one. If they work, put them back in the cup. If they don't work, throw them out. This is a simple task you can do while doing something else. It really is easy, and there is a great feeling for completing a task like this, no matter how small or seemingly insignificant.

What little messes or 'pen cups' do you have around the house that you could clean up, sort, whatever, while you are just sitting around? List them here:

Painless Multitasking

In the previous section, we talked about the Pen Cup Exercise. When you do something like this, you are in fact multitasking—switching off between one tedious, mindless task (sorting) and another mindless task that's fun and doesn't require 100% of your attention (watching TV, listening to music, talking on the phone).

This is a great way to handle the boring tasks in your life. Here are a few ideas:

☐ **Folding laundry**—If you're like a lot of us, washing laundry is one thing, folding it is another. Why not just dump all of the clean laundry on the couch and fold it while you're watching TV on Netflix?

☐ **Clean out a drawer**—Dump out a drawer on the coffee table while you're listening to music. Keep a trash can nearby, and toss out the crap you don't need. Organize the stuff that's left, and you'll be able to find the things you need quickly.

☐ **Roll your coins**—Hopefully, you've been putting all your change in a big jar, and it's not all over the house, in the couch, on the car floor. Watching a game on TV is a perfect time to sort and roll your coins—and, you'll have a nice chunk of spending money to boot.

☐ **Sort through stacks of paper**—If you have done any of the 15-minute clean ups, you may have a stack of papers that needs sorting. Watching TV or listening to music is a perfect time to do this. Just get a bag to put recycling in, recycle what you don't need, and make separate stacks for bills, important papers to file, things to follow up on, and so forth. Then—put them where they belong!

☐ **Clean out your backpack, your purse, your wallet**—Crazy as it seems, I've been known to clean out my purse while waiting at the doctor's office. What else are you going to do besides read four-year-old magazines? It's simple, and it's easy, and you may just find money you thought you lost. Worth it? You bet!

What annoying tasks can you take care of when you're watching TV, listening to music, or just relaxing?

Organizing Your Personal Workspace

At the beginning of this chapter, we talked about your ideal workspace, and now we're going to return to that exercise and do it again. You can see now that everyone needs at least one personal workspace where they can sit down, know where everything is, and get some work done. This does not have to be a desk—it could be the kitchen table, your briefcase, any physical location where you know where everything is. And depending on what sort of work you do, it may not be a flat surface at all. If you are a traveling salesperson and always on the road, then your car might be your personal workspace. Remember, the where doesn't matter—it's all in how you set it up.

So, imagine for a moment what you need to do your work or studies. Should it be a quiet place, or can you handle (or maybe even need) a little background noise? What tools do you need? Computer, internet, printer? Or maybe an artist's sketchbook or lots of binder paper? Do you want to have a phone handy or will it just distract you? What other considerations should be made?

First, list the 'must-have' items you need to do your work:

1.

2.

3.

4.

5.

Next, list the things that would be *useful*—and not distracting—in getting your job done.

1. _____

2. _____

3. _____

4. _____

5. _____

Finally, redraw your ideal workspace now that you have learned a little about organization and distraction. When you are done, compare it with your original drawing from earlier in the chapter. How is it different?

MY WORKSPACE

Your Space Management Profile

Now that you've learned the key points of space management, take the time to go back through this chapter, and make some notes about what your space management profile is:

My Most Lost Items and Where They Belong:	
1.	
2.	
3.	
4.	
5.	

Areas of Chaos in the Home/Office and Plan to Change:	
1.	
2.	
3.	
4.	
5.	

What Mindless Tasks Can I Do When Relaxing?

1.

2.

3.

4.

5.

Virtual Management

So far, we've talked about how to manage your time, how to manage your physical space, and now we're going to venture into another realm—virtual management. This is especially important if you are:

- ❏ A student
- ❏ A writer
- ❏ A business person

Or…

- ❏ Ever use a computer or any sort of filing system somewhere in your life

In short, *you*.

While the focus of this section is using a computer, this information also applies to the 'physical' version of computers—file folders, index cards, binders, calendars, and so forth. All of these are ways that we keep information in 'piles'—and as you can guess, we sort this information in the same ways we sort other things—'like with like,' frequent use, reminder items, and so forth. The differences are two: one, we frequently don't think how we store things in the virtual realm (bad on us!); and two, how we sort things can help—or hinder—how we process information, which in turn can help or hurt our cognitive performance. More on that later.

Visual Organization

To start, let's have a look at a couple of screen shots of a computer desktop.

So, what's on this person's desktop? Even though it's hard to read, you can see that there are lots of shortcuts, random files and folders, and a bunch of files that are named in such a way that it would be easy to forget what they are. Kind of a mess. Now, let's look at the same desktop on the next page.

A different story, right? First off, the virtual desktop is arranged a bit more neatly, new file folders were created for a bunch of the accumulated files and short cuts. And, all of the random files are gone—hopefully either thrown away or filed in their proper places.

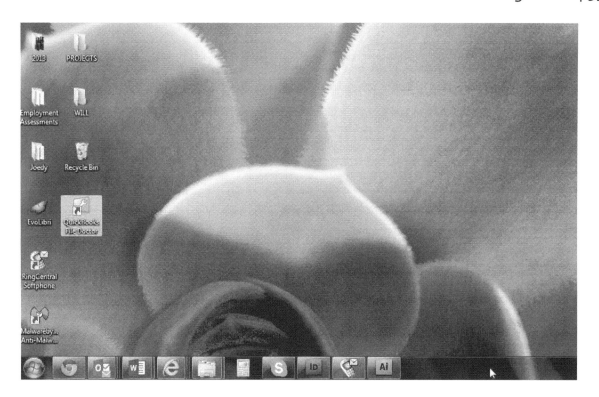

Now, let's look at a folder from my desktop that's gotten a bit out of control.

While you probably can't make out the detail, it should be clear that I have lots of folders that are clearly named so that I can quickly identify what I'm looking for. But I also have a bunch of loose files that need to be filed and reorganized, and a bunch of duplicate files from a backup restoration. Messy, messy!

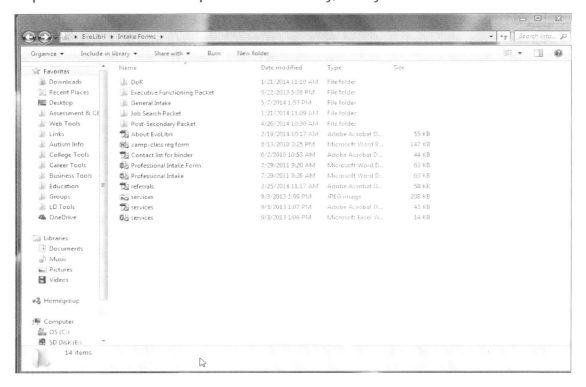

Once they are cleaned up in the above screen shot, it makes it very easy to find what I'm looking for. It makes it a lot easier to see what's there. I have made new folders, and have combined some of the higher level folders into other existing folders—so that I don't have to slog through so much information to find what I'm looking for.

Some Theory on Why This Works

This all may seem just silly—who cares how messy our computer desktops are? Does it really matter if I have my files scattered all over the place? Well, actually, it does matter—we can more easily find things if we consistently put them in the same place, we can more easily remember where things are if they are stored 'like with like', and for some important additional reasons relating to our internal processing, as discussed below:

❑ **Seven, plus or minus two**—A cognitive psychologist named George Miller published a paper in 1956 called *The Magical Number Seven, Plus or Minus Two* that described how the brain can store seven things—plus or minus two—in working memory.[1] This research has heavily influenced the theory of instructional design and computer user interface design in the intervening decades. (As an interesting note, Miller also coined the term 'chunking' which we'll talk about later.) While the precise number has been bandied about in recent years (the 'magic' number may actually be lower than seven), it is certainly true that our working memory is limited and thus, we should try to 'chunk' our information into smallish groups for easier retrieval. I have more than seven folders in the picture above, but I think you can see that it is much easier to go through than the previous mess! Try to keep your folders and your desktop clean, and down to seven or nine items for easy retrieval.

❑ **Form and Color**—A later and equally influential cognitive theory by Robert Logie entitled *Visuo-Spatial Working Memory*[2] states that information stored in working memory can be forgotten (the memory trace is lost), reinforced (the memory trace is recalled enough times so that the memory trace is sustained), or that the memory trace will be overwritten by a new memory. He also asserts that in visually-based systems (as is our computer desktop), memory is hampered by "irrelevant material."[3] Logie also states that shape and color, if used as semantic encoding (giving additional meaning to an object to help in later recall), were used, we would be able to more easily access our own information. For this reason, it is useful to use different colors for groups of items, such as the color red for deadline items, different shapes for other items, such as folders, and so on. This type of encoding—sort of a primal metadata—helps us sort and remember where information is.

❑ **Placement coding**—Logie's theory also suggests that where we put things—or where they exist in space—can help or hinder our ability to access them, and it's reasonable to assume that this applies to both virtual and 'real-life' objects. Drivers know that it takes a bit of time to adjust to a new car where the windshield wipers are on the left if they are used to them on the right, because they have to 'remap' their brains to remember where the tool is now. And, when you organize your physical workspace, you may always keep your phone on the right (or left if you are left-handed), and maybe your highlighter pens on the left of your desk. On your computer desktop, you can place folders and applications

---

1   Miller, G. (1956). The magical number seven, plus or minus two: Some limits on our capacity for processing information. *The Psychological Review*, 1956, vol. 63, pp. 81-97.

2   Logie, R. (1995). *Visuo-spatial Working Memory*. Lawrence Erlbaum Associates, Hillsdale, AZ, pp. 64-92

3   Ibid., p. 74

wherever you want—the key is consistency, so that your brain 'knows' exactly where to drag the mouse when you want to access a specific item. If you are consistent with where you put things, again, your brain can more easily remember where things are, and can work more efficiently and quickly.

Putting It into Practice

Now you have a little better understanding of why creating 'calm out of chaos' is actually an important tool. Let's go one step further and show you how this works and how you can apply it.

Take a look at the calendar below. Boring, bland, and hard to scan. This is how most people's calendars look, which is one reason why it's hard to get into the habit of looking at it every day. How is your brain going to store this information? It's just a bunch of random information.

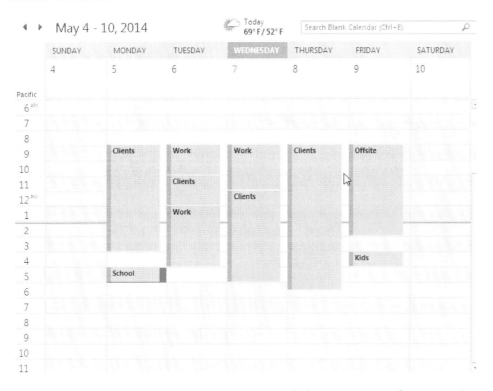

There are a lot more than seven things and there are very few visual cues here, other than that the items are sorted by day and time. That's probably not enough encoding for your brain, and so it will likely not hang on to much of this information—except things like your classes, because those repeat. But the dentist appointment? Going to the gym? Even something fun could easily be forgotten.

Now, let's look below. What happens when you look at this version of the same week? Even though the rendition you are looking at is grayscale (the original is in color of course), everything is simpler to see, isn't it? Things 'pop' more because they are colored—so even if the color were random, it would still help your brain hang on to this information.

But, the color isn't random—in the example below, Dark Blue are classes, Light Green is homework, Dark Gray is the Gym, Purple are fun activities, and Yellow means that something must be done before that activity—such as remembering to bring your insurance card to the dentist or buying Sarah a birthday present.

This color tagging, available in all commercial software calendars, helps your brain encode the information it sees so that you can remember it later, and the way the information is now broken up makes it generally easier to scan.

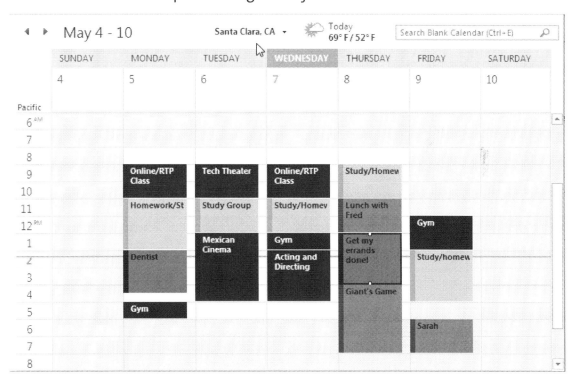

So, by looking at this calendar on Sunday night, you would be 'telling' your brain "get the insurance card and put it in my wallet, and don't forget Sarah's birthday present! Oh, and cool! I have lunch with Fred and a Giant's game this week!" The non-colored calendar relies on text and placement coding only. Can you see what adding another layer of coding information (color by type of activity) to this data does in terms of usability—and 'rememberability'?

Now, a quick tip—most calendaring systems allow you to use color, and some applications (MS Outlook) allow you to create algorithms that will apply colors to certain events. For example, the terms 'dentist' and 'doctor' in my Outlook creates a yellow record, and anything with the term 'lunch' or 'dinner' creates a purple record automatically. Even cooler is the fact that many Smartphones will 'carry' the colors when you sync your calendar to your phone, making your phone's calendar very easy to read as well.

Using color to encode information is very helpful, but you can also use symbols. For example, you may have noticed a few pages back that the icon for my work folder is a butterfly—because a butterfly is part of my logo. This makes it really easy for me to see on my computer desktop, no matter how cluttered it has gotten. You can also easily set this up on your PC computer desktop by right-clicking the item on your desktop, selecting *Properties*, and then *Customize*.

I can always find my work folder, now, no matter how much stuff has accumulated on my desktop. In fact, I ordered custom debit and credit cards for my company with my butterfly logo on them—not because it's cool (okay, that was part of it), but so that I could easily identify them in my wallet.

You can use this sort of color and symbolic encoding to organize your digital life, but remember, too much of a good thing is just too much. If you have too many items on your desktop, it won't matter (and may even hurt) if they are multicolored shapes— your brain will be overloaded and it will be hard to pick them out—remember the *I Spy* books with photographs with hundreds of items, and you had to find just a few? It's the same thing. Less is more!

How can you use color, symbols, and placement to help your brain organize?

ThoughtBox: Using Your Computer to Organize Your Mind

As crazy it as it may sound, you can try using your computer to organize your mind so that it can more effectively process information unconsciously.

Cognitive psychologists know that we process a great deal of information unconsciously, and that information moves from our unconscious (or preconscious) to our conscious minds.[1] An example of this is when we wake up with the solution to a problem we had the day before—our preconscious brains have been working on the problem while we slept, and 'delivered' the answer to our conscious minds when we awoke. Additionally, information that is conscious can become preconscious, or automatic. Driving is a good example of this. When we first learn to drive, we are very conscious of what we are doing—in fact, we are hyper-vigilant, or overly conscious. Over a period of time, driving becomes automatic. We no longer think about carefully moving to the right lane—we simply do it.

There's a lot of potential processing our brains could be doing if we only primed it to do so. Here's a way you can try to make the most of your preconscious processing:

1. Clean up your computer desktop and organize your file folders as we discussed earlier in this chapter.

2. Create a folder that is just for your work.

3. In that folder, create subfolders. The idea is to sort out different types of work (remember how our brains like to sort) and create a hierarchy. For example, if you are working on creative projects, you might name these subfolders *Ideas*, *Work in Progress*, *Completed*.

4. Your subfolders should contain your actual project files, and they should have descriptive names (like, *Tasker Account*, not *1-2-11*).

In this way, you have set aside a virtual location for your mind to 'store' things as it processes information in the background throughout the day.

---

1   Dehaene, S., et al. (2006). Conscious, preconscious, and subliminal processing: A testable taxonomy. *Trends in Cognitive Science*. Vol 10(5): 204-11

If you have tried the exercise in the ThoughtBox above, you have created a virtual—and visual—hierarchy of your work. This will definitely keep you more organized, but may also give your brain a place to 'put' information as you process it. When you work on that project next, your preconscious mind can pass 'solutions' to your conscious mind regarding this project in a more orderly fashion. I have had several clients use this method with excellent results. It may be that just the organization helps them focus, but they claim that it also helps them harness their preconscious processing.

Try it and see if it works for you—what are some projects or areas of your life that you would like your mind to work on, and how can you set up a virtual location on your computer to facilitate that work?

Creating virtual organization is something we do all the time. The extent to which we use this organization in a more conscious way is what makes us better and more effective at doing the things we set out to do. We have all heard that we don't use 90% of our brains. I don't think that's true. What I do believe is that we don't realize how much more effective we can be in our lives if we set upon our tasks with purpose. In the end, it really is about being mindful of what we hope to do with our lives.

Your Virtual Management Profile

Virtual management is something most of us do without thinking—and that is part of the problem. Our computer desktops, our calendars, our email, all cry out for a way for us to use them more effectively. Let's look at some ways you can do just that.

Ways that I Can Use Color, Placement, Symbols On My Computer	
1.	
2.	
3.	
4.	
5.	

Ways that I Can Use Color, Placement, Symbols On My Calendar	
1.	
2.	
3.	
4.	
5.	

Ways that I Can Use Color, Placement, Symbols in Other Areas of My Life	
1.	
2.	
3.	
4.	
5.	

Finally, try your hand at drawing a picture of your brain without clutter, but able to do what it has been longing to do—happily process information effectively and efficiently for you while you go about your day!

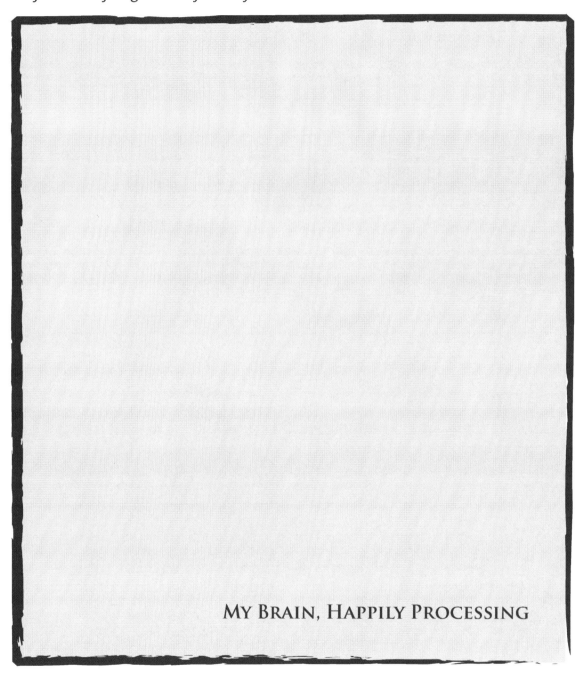

MY BRAIN, HAPPILY PROCESSING

Memory Management

We've covered a lot of skills so far that relate in part to how we 'manage' our memory, by using cues, colors, placement, and so forth, but it's worth exploring memory a bit further—how it works, its impact on learning and executive functioning, and how to improve it.

How Memory Works

Memory, as it turns out, is a very complicated process. But for our purposes here, we can talk about it as having distinct phases (acquisition, storage, and retrieval of information) and as being one of three types (sensory or accidental memory, long-term memory or remembering, and working memory or knowing). Understanding how your memory works may in turn help you use your memory to better affect, and help you understand what you can do to improve it and its effectiveness.

Memory Phases

We acquire a 'to-be' memory through one of our senses. We may forever remember the way our grandmother's gingerbread smells, or the sound of our first child's laughter. We might be able to remember the way a pet's fur feels, or the color our tree turns in the fall.

But, we experience a great deal through our senses every day, and not everything is stored as a retrievable memory. In order for a retrievable memory to be formed, the information must be encoded as it is stored.

Encoding is a way that our brain associates the memory with other information that builds a 'breadcrumb path' back to the memory for later retrieval. For example, the smell of grandmother's gingerbread may be associated in my memory with typically-related information such as Christmas, cookies, and baking. But this smell may also be encoded with emotional or sensory information such as being warm, feeling happy, snow falling, and the 'wet-dog' smell of my grandfather's dog Max. This is why a single memory can have such a power impact on us—and floods us with feeling or related memories. Indeed, there is quite a bit of evidence that demonstrates that those memories associated with a powerful emotion are often much 'stronger' and easier to access.[1]

Sometimes we are more deliberate—and conscious—in how we encode events or information, such as when we are studying. When we are in class or in a business meeting, we take notes, we highlight passages in papers we read, and we memorize certain information. When we were in elementary school, we may have been taught simple mnemonics to help us memorize information (My [Mercury] Very [Venus] Educated [Earth] Mother [Mars] Just [Jupiter] Served [Saturn] Us [Uranus] Pizza [Pluto, which has since been relegated to the more lowly status of a dwarf planet]).

Retrieval of memories can be dicey, as anyone can tell you—"It's on the tip of my tongue," or "I used to know that!" are common phrases, while we might be able to quickly recall our first phone number decades after we last dialed it, or the name of our preschool teacher, whom we haven't seen in many years. Some memories are 'at the ready' for immediate use, such as our phone number or our best friend's name—those memories are stored in what is called *working memory*. Other memories are less accessible, and stored more deeply in our mind. To some degree, this is a 'use it or lose it' proposition—there is evidence that the more frequently we use a memory, the stronger it becomes.[2] This is why repetitive studying of information can help us pass our upcoming test.

Learning—Purposeful Encoding

When we are studying for a test, memorizing our lines in a play, reviewing a presentation we are about to give, we are attempting to encode the information in such a way as to facilitate recall later—why else would we spend hours writing up Cornell notes on the war of 1812 or reviewing flashcards of the periodic table? When we study we are attempting to purposefully encode the information we are absorbing so that we can later recall it, typically for an examination of some sort.

---

1   Cahill, L., and McGaugh, JL. (1998). Mechanisms of emotional arousal and lasting declarative memory. *Trends in Neuroscience*. Jul; 21(7):249-9.

2   Erickson, M. and Reder, M. (1998). The effects of multiple repetitions on implicit memory across long durations. Department of Psychology, Carnegie Mellon University, Pittsburgh, PA. Unpublished manuscript.

Typically, encoding takes one of a variety of formats:

❑ **Simple reading**—just as it sounds, this is simply reading text to understand the content. When we are reading a novel or a magazine, we are not necessarily concerned about committing details to memory, but instead to understand the larger story, and generally, simple reading will do this. Note that some people who have very good working or intrinsic memory can read a complicated text and just 'get it.' This has less to do with native intelligence and more to do with exceptional memory function!

❑ **Note-taking and highlighting**—this is the next level of encoding for most of us. We highlight key words or passages in a book for later review, or we will write down notes about what we are reading, in the margins of the book or in a notebook. There is a distinct problem with this, however—many people have difficulty knowing what to highlight or what to write notes about.

❑ **Review of notes, study guides, handouts**—after having read the text and taken the notes, most students will go back and review what they have written or highlighted, and may also use study guides handed out by the teachers to prompt specific learning or memorization. This is often referred to as 'cramming' where you are literally trying to cram all of this information into your working memory so that it will be easily and quickly available during a test. The problem with cramming is—it doesn't work well. You have limited working memory, and there is only so much you can 'commit to memory' in a short period of time, because cramming is not the same as learning.

❑ **Practicing**—some types of learning require physical practice, such as speaking a foreign language, learning calligraphy, or pitching a fast ball. All of these are a combination of recalling the steps you need to take, and then practicing the physical movements needed to complete the action. For some things we practice, such as learning a foreign language, this is a combination of recall of the information and the muscle memory of executing the sounds.

❑ **Memorization**—some information we have to memorize in order to access it during a test or exam, or for later purposes, such as memorizing our math facts. What we are really doing when we memorize something is we are consciously trying to move information from explicit (remembering) to implicit (knowing) memory.

Knowing Vs. Remembering

Some things we seem to just know. We don't have to labor to retrieve the information from our memory, it is just there for most of us—how to make toast, what shoe size we are, the names of our children or parents, what two plus two is. We *know* this information. Other information takes a bit more information to retrieve—our social security number, a particularly difficult algorithm from Trigonometry, where we left our keys!

These two states are called **implicit** (knowing) and **explicit** (remembering) memory, and as you can undoubtedly guess, consciously studying a subject and learning content generally falls under the area of explicit memory. We are explicitly committing information to our memory. The interesting bit here is how some information, over time, moves from implicit to explicit memory. There was a time in everyone's life when two plus two was something you had to remember—and then it wasn't. You simply *knew* this to be true.

Do you remember how that came to be? If like most kids you were repeatedly drilled on your arithmetic facts in the second or third grade (explicit learning) until you simply knew them (implicit memory, aka working memory). As a commentary on our current educational system, one could question how much we actual know by the time we graduate high school or college. Is what we do learning, or remembering? It is also interesting to note that by and large the cognitive decline seen in the elderly is most clearly (and first) evident in the area of explicit memory—recall, or remembering.

When you are studying or learning a new topic, be aware that you are purposefully encoding the information you are taking in. Learning is rarely a passive activity: you start a study session with self-awareness that you are actively engaging with the material in such a fashion as to commit it to memory. How you go about studying—committing information to memory—will have a significant impact on your ability to retain the information. Additionally, we also know that your emotional state—how you feel about the subject you are studying—has an impact on how well you can encode the information. In short, if you hate biology, it will be that much harder to learn it.

Multi-Modal Learning

As you can see, learning—or, consciously committing to memory—is a bit of a dicey exercise, depending on your emotional state, the study tools you use, and the amount of time you have to commit information to memory.

But, there are other ways that can help you 'purposefully encode' information so that you can use it and recall it at a later time. One of the most powerful ways to do this is to use multi-modal learning techniques. Remember how in previous sections we talked about how your brain brings in information through a variety of different channels—visual, auditory, sensory, and so forth? Well, as it turns out, using these various channels to encode memory helps to reinforce the learning, because you are actively engaging all of your senses, which creates multiple links to the information. Not just one—what did I read? But—what did I read, listen to, look at, and practice? Can you see why that would help?

By using a multi-modal approach to learning, we are "(1) promoting learning by providing an external representation of the (2) deeper processing of information; and (3) maintaining learner attention by making the information more attractive and motivating, hence making complex information easier to comprehend."[3] Feel free to share this little gem with your Organic Chemistry professor who seems to think that you should learn this information from his droning voice and a series of ill-designed, black and white Powerpoint slides! This is passive learning at its worst—and it does not work well.

We know that multi-modal teaching works much better, and that students who learn in this fashion "outperform students who learn using traditional approaches with single modes."[4] The good news is that you can create a multi-modal approach to your encoding strategies, even if your teachers and professors do not.

Visual Memory

We remember pictures much better than words, probably because we have only had language for a relatively short period of time, and so our brains are more keen on identifying and storing visual information. This is known as 'picture superiority effect,' where "...visual memory performance typically exceeds that of memory for

---

3   Shah, P., & Freedman, E. G. (2003). Visuospatial cognition in electronic learning. *Journal of Educational Computing Research*, 29(3), 315-324.

4   Fadel, C. (2008). *Multimodal Learning Through Media: What the Research Says*. San Jose, CA: Cisco Systems. Page 16.

words."[5] Think about something you've learned, in part or whole, visually, such as the Periodic Table. When you think about a specific chemical on that chart, do you visualize where it lives on that chart? Where it is, what it is next to? The Periodic Table was devised in that fashion for this very purpose—the categorization, the colors, and the visual representation itself aids in recall. Chemistry majors who have committed this information to memory know where silver is on the table, and know why it is in that location.

Auditory Memory

As with visual memory, this is memory that is retrieved based on an auditory cue. And, we use it all the time, whether we are conscious of it or not. Think about your cell phone. Do you have different ring tones for different people? Different chimes for different events? What happens when you hear a horn honk, or a fire alarm go off? All of these events are closely tied to an auditory memory—you had to learn what they mean at some point.

We additionally 'learn' far more subtle information that comes to us through aural channels—as children, most of us quickly learn that the tone of our parent's voice can mean they are happy, sad, or angry—and how to act accordingly. We know that tone in our mother's voice!

Muscle Memory

Muscle memory, or motor learning, is how our brains encode information around a certain physical task. We use this type of memory every time we type, we play a video game or a musical instrument, roll an 'r' in Spanish, drive a car, or ride a bike. Because we have repeatedly practiced, our bodies 'know' what to do—we are not consciously aware of the numerous, specific movements our bodies are making to execute the task. We learned all of these tasks by practice—at one point, we were keenly aware of learning the task by explicit learning, until the skill became implicit. We no longer had to remember—we knew.

Olfactory Memory

Olfactory memory is considered to be the most primal form of memory in humans. In fact, we develop this type of memory before we are born, and can recognize at some level the smell of the amniotic fluid we floated in before birth and can also recognize

5   Williams, C. (2010). Incidental and intentional visual memory: What memories are and are not affected by encoding tasks? *Visual Cognition*, 18:9, pp. 1349.

the smell of our mother's breasts and breast milk.[6] Pheromones drive attraction to mates, the smell of smoke causes us to take notice, food that has gone bad puts off an unpleasant aroma. Our survival depended on us being able to recognize safety, danger, and the potential for procreation based on smell. These are things we came to know in order to survive.

Using Multi-Modal Approaches in Studying

As you can see, we use all of our senses to learn information—to commit information to memory. However, some learning is best attained through specific channels. It would be difficult to learn how to play the violin without ever picking up the instrument, and it would be difficult for most of us to learn the Periodic Table by having it recited to us.

Having said that, we can most effectively learn how to play the violin by listening to how great artists have mastered a given piece, by studying music theory, and by learning to read music. We can most effectively memorize the Periodic Table by understanding how the table was organized, how elements relate to each other, and maybe even by visualizing the glint of gold or having encountered the distinct aroma of ammonia.

We can think about multi-modal learning channels as having direct and supportive effects on our attempt to encode information to memory:

❑ **Visual (direct)**—visual learning can simply be reading, but other types of visual stimuli may be better at helping you learn. Videos, films and multimedia presentations on the topic in question will help, as will flashcards and well-designed graphics and tables on the material. Additionally, drawing tables and graphics, and writing notes ourselves seem to be very effective in committing the information to memory—this makes sense as it draws on two approaches—visual—watching as we do—and the act of writing and drawing.

❑ **Auditory (direct)**—listening to a lecturer explain a topic is one of the primary ways we are taught, and for many of us, it is a good way to learn unless you have impairment in auditory processing. Even if we are good auditory learners, most of us will also need to take notes on the lecture. This not only saves the key pieces of information for us to study later, but as noted above, the act of writing things down aids in memory formation. Additional methods to try for

---

6   Varendi, H., Christensson, K., Porter, H., Winberg, J. (1997). Soothing effect of amniotic fluid smell in new-born infants. *Early Human Development* 51: 47-55.

strong auditory learners is to listen to recorded information, such as listening to a text book downloaded from Learning Ally while following along with the text in front of you.

❑ **Auditory (supportive)**—for individuals who have auditory sensitivity or attentional challenges, using screening auditory input may help with focus so that the other senses can do their jobs in relaying the content to the brain for memory formation. This comes in the form of listening to music at a low level to screen out the intrusive noises, or by listening to white (or pink or brown) noise to do the same. We know that music can also improve our mood, so listening to music that lifts our spirits (improving our emotional state) without intruding on the learning process, would likely help anyone learn material more effectively.

❑ **Motor (supportive)**—for most academic topics, motor learning can only provide supportive effect on the memory formation. However, as with visual learning, motor learning can be a great support to the learning process. Typing or writing notes are both physical activities that appear to promote learning. Drawing tables and charts works in the same way—you are manipulating the information. Additionally, for those with attentional issues, doodling, chewing gum, manipulating a fidget, or tapping a pencil all seem to help maintain the attentional state needed for learning.

❑ **Olfactory (supportive)**—learning by smell is not something we can generally accomplish for high school and college classes, sadly. But, we can use our olfactory senses to help set the stage for learning, much as using music or sound. Certainly, learning will be inhibited if we are sitting in a room overcome by garlic or exhaust smells, and it makes sense the reverse is probably true. If we are in an environment imbued with aromas with which we have a pleasant association, we are more likely to be in a happier emotional state,[7] and thus, will be able to learn more readily. Most people have better focus when smelling citrus, mint, and certain herbal or woodsy aromas (rosemary, basil, cedar, pine, eucalyptus), and report feeling calm when smelling certain floral and other herbal aromas (lavender, patchouli, rose). Aromatherapy, anyone?

---

7   Herz, R. (2005). Odor-associative Learning and Emotion: Effects on Perception and Behavior, *Chemical Senses*, 30 (suppl 1): i250-i251.

Increasing Memory When Learning

Now that we've learned a bit about how memory works and a few ways that we can increase our capacity to learn, let's look at a few other ways that we can enhance the explicit encoding of information—learn!

Pre-Reading

Before undertaking that next chapter in your beloved edition of University Physics with Modern Physics (which a quick Google search noted as 'one of the most difficult textbooks' ever, and at the bargain rate of $225), plan your attack. One way to do this is as follows:

1. Get your notebook out, start a clean page, and write down the chapter name at the top.

2. Write *Key Terms* on the left side of the page.

3. Read the chapter introduction, if available.

4. Write down key terms that come up in the introduction.

5. Write *Learning Objectives* on the left side of the page, below your key terms.

6. Read the chapter summary, if available.

7. Write down what you were supposed to have learned in the chapter—which will likely be described in the summary (and possibly the introduction as well).

Review the above information before you start reading. Really understand what information you are trying to pour into your brain before you begin, so that your brain can look for the information it now knows you want it to learn. This 'priming' helps us form appropriate memory on given topics if "they were defined prior to the search":[8]

> "When a search target is encountered, the participant must identify and remember it as the object that is searched for...[thus there is]...a difference in the encoding episode of the target objects. [This in turn]...can influence not only the initial processing of the objects, but also the memories of that result."[9]

---

8   Williams, C. (2010). Incidental and intentional visual memory: What memories are and are not affected by encoding tasks? *Visual Cognition*, 18:9, pp. 1349., pp. 1363.
9   Ibid., 1365.

Make sure you ascertain what you are trying to learn before you actually try do it—being mindful that the task we are trying to achieve is indeed part of the task itself.

Note-Taking

As we discussed earlier, note-taking seems to help in large part by giving us a multimodal way of encoding information and storing it into memory. However, note-taking is also a very useful way of:

1. Recording the location of a specific piece of information, useful when studying or writing papers later; and,

2. Processing or 'manipulating' the information, which also helps encoding.

So, in our previous example of pre-reading, we started a page for the chapter we are reading. We wrote down the key terms and the learning objectives. As we read along, we should stop every so often, certainly after a difficult paragraph or section, and write down what the passage is saying in our own words. This use of expressive language—grabbing the meaning through cognition, and saying it again—is one of the most vital ways to encode memory and to facilitate learning.

If you merely write down what the author wrote, it will help in learning, but not nearly as much as rephrasing it: "The more the information learning process involves understanding and transformation operations, the greater the intensity and effectiveness of the learning process." [10]

If you find it difficult to write any notes on what you are reading, it is most likely because you are not learning. If this is the case, go back to your notebook, review what you should be learning, and check what you read against the learning objectives. That is what you should be learning, and the material you should be putting 'into your own words' in your notes.

Highlighting

Highlighting information we are reading does help us recall the information, and aids as a study tool when we review the information at a later time.

However, many people have difficulty ascertaining what they should highlight Consequently, you might see someone's used text book that is practically glowing with

---

10   Boch, F. & Piolat, A. (2005). Note taking and learning: a summary of research. *The WAC Journal,* Vol. 16: September 2005. pp 101-113.

yellow ink, or you might see another with very little highlighting at all. Others still will use different colors to highlight different types on information in a single book.

As you might guess, this last form of highlighting is probably the most effective, as we are not just randomly encoding information, but doing it with purpose. For example, if you are reading Wuthering Heights for an advanced literature class, you might use the following color coding as you read along:

- ❏ Symbolism, Allegory, Imagery—pink
- ❏ Narrator PoV—blue
- ❏ Tone and Setting—green
- ❏ Plot twists—purple

Again, this requires that you think about what you are looking for before you start! On your notebook page, write down what you are looking for, and how you will encode it. Other categories to highlight could be key terms, dates, references, discussion, and so forth. Know what you are looking for in the material!

Manipulating the Information

You may have heard the expression that the best way to learn information is to teach it, and this is certainly the case. Once you understand information well enough so that you can explain it in your own words, you have pretty much mastered it.

This is why study groups are useful, why it is important to take notes that are not just copying from the text or regurgitating what the professor says, and yes, why homework and classwork and writing papers actually do help you learn.

All of these tasks demand that you manipulate the information in some way. The information is not just lying there statically in your brain, but is being used. And when it comes to memory and recall, it really is a use it or lose it proposition.

More importantly, though, manipulation of the information ensures that we have learned the content, that it has meaning to us, it is not just stored as random information to be recalled for a quiz in two days.

Timing

Timing is important in terms of studying and encoding memories. We talked about your own best times to learn, when you are generally most alert and when you are tired, and about the times of day best suited for incoming input through reading, such as earlier in the day, and when most people are better at expressing knowledge through writing, usually later in the day. We know that most of us cannot learn non-stop for hours on end, because our brains need time to process what we are learning, store the memories, and yes, just rest before we assault them again with more information.

Additionally, there is considerable research showing that the best times to reinforce previous learning is to study the content between one and 24 hours of its initial presentation. This means that even if all you have time for is to jot down some notes, review your textbook, or chat with a classmate for a few minutes after lecture, you will be aiding your brain in encoding the information. Better yet would be actual studying of the material for 20 to 30 minutes.

Also, in terms of timing—it's never a good idea to try to sit for hours at a time to study. Follow these guidelines:

- ❑ Break studying into 30 minute chunks, after which you should get up, stretch, get a drink of water, go to the bathroom.
- ❑ Take longer breaks (10-30 minutes) when you start to lose focus.
- ❑ Stop studying and eat, rest, or play when you are no longer able to focus at all.
- ❑ Follow your own biorhythms to the extent possible by studying the subjects that work the best for you at varying times of day.
- ❑ Eat enough protein and vegetables. Try to stay away from carbs and massive amounts of caffeine.
- ❑ Get enough sleep! Even if you can't get a full eight hours, try to cat nap in the midday to catch up. Just don't sleep longer than 90-120 minutes. One REM cycle is perfect, two is too much and will likely interrupt your normal sleep pattern.

Retrieval Repetition

One of the best ways to encode information into memory is by simply practicing retrieval of the information. This is what flashcards do, what quizzes and tests do—they allow us to practice accessing the information, and the more we retrieve it, the stronger the memory trace is, and the more the information moves from 'remembering' to 'knowing.' This, more than other more elaborate strategies like concept mapping, significantly aids in learning difficult subjects such as lab sciences and math.[11]

As much as we may hate them, those study questions at the end of the chapters in our text books are one of the best ways we have to learn. And the best time to do them, is very soon after we have read the chapter.

About Invasive Memories and Thoughts

Unlike learning with intent, some memories are formed through trauma of one sort or another, and come to our mind unbidden, causing us stress, anxiety, or sadness. Needless to say, these memories can inhibit the formation of new memories, as we are flooded with negative emotions that essentially prohibit learning. Your mind and body are solely focused on the 'attack'—real or imagined—and are primed to that battle.

In a more gentle form, drifting thoughts, perseverating on past failures, on allowing our mind to 'go to' the thoughts of the ultimate stupidity of learning the information in front of us, will all significantly impede the learning process. Even our personality traits may have some impact on how we learn.[12]

Know this. Really understand it. If you cannot 'switch off' the internal channel inside your head that is repeating all of the reasons why you cannot do what you are trying to do, then you need to stop and take a break. Learning has ceased.

Know that you are done for the moment, and sitting there screaming at your textbook or Excel spreadsheet will not move you forward. But, you can work on the thoughts: take a walk, write affirmations, watch a movie. Do something that you know will improve your mood. Try 'pushing' the invasive memories or thoughts out of your mind, by closing your eyes, and imagine gently pushing them until they float away. Change your environment so that you can change your mood so that learning can once again occur.

Many of us have 'automatic thoughts' or memories—what are yours? Write them down and understand why they come to you. If you find yourself stuck a lot, find a

11   J. D. Karpicke, & J. R. Blunt. Retrieval Practice Produces More Learning than Elaborative Studying with Concept Mapping. *Science,* 2011; DOI: 10.1126/science.1199327

12   Dweck, C. and Leggett, E. (1988). A social-cognitive approach to motivation and personality. *Psychological Review,* Vol. 95(2), 256-273.

ThoughtBox: A Note on Thin-Slicing

As brought to national attention in Malcolm Gladwell's best-selling book *Blink*, we have the ability to use 'rapid cognition' where "our unconscious is able to find patterns in situations and behavior based on very narrow slices of experience."[12]

Why is this useful? Because it allows us to make confident, valid decisions based on the aggregate information we bring to each new situation. This, perhaps obviously, works best when you are making decisions that are similar to decisions you have made in the past.

For example, if you have bought hundreds of pairs of shoes and know what styles fit you well and which pinch your toes, you can look at a dozen shoes and know which ones are likely to fit. That's thin-slicing.

Thin-slicing does require that you have been observant in the decisions that you have made in the past, that you have recognized patterns, even if only unconsciously. All of the information you have gathered before comes to bear when you make a new decision, which may be why when you are faced with something completely new and unique, it feels so overwhelming. You have not gathered any data on this yet, and have to start fresh.

There is a downside to thin-slicing, and it can cause us to make poor decisions based on prejudice—both positive and negative. If we are socialized—as many of us are—to believe that tall, dark, and handsome equals success and honesty, you may not dig deeply enough beneath the surface when making a judgment on a person's character, and may pick whomever 'looks' the part.

On the flip side, if our least-favorite teacher was very thin, we may decide that all thin people are always mean-spirited. In short, while thin-slicing can be a very good way to made rapid decisions, we have to be careful to not let prejudice creep in.

---

12   Gladwell, M. (2005). *Blink*. Little, Brown and Company, New York, NY. pp. 32.

Your Memory Management Profile

We've gone through some additional information about how memory works and how we learn. Using that information, go through the table below and create your memory profile:

How I can use multi-modal learning	
Visual	
Auditory	
Olfactory	
Kinesthetic (muscle)	
How I can use other tools to be more effective when learning	
Pre-reading	
Highlighting	
Manipulating information	
Timing	
Repetition	
Ways I can handle 'invasive thoughts'	
Change my environment	
Change my mood	
Change my perception	
Push the thoughts away	

My Automatic Thoughts

Section II

Project Management

Information Management

Thought Management

Obstacle Management

The CEO of Self

Project Management

What does project management have to do with executive functioning? Let's take a look at the definition of project management from Wikipedia:[1]

> *Project management is the discipline of planning, organizing, securing and managing resources to bring about the successful completion of specific project goals and objectives.*

Cool. Now, let's think about some of things you might want to do in a given year:

- ❑ **Plant a vegetable garden**—First, you'll have to decide where you'll plant your garden, then figure out if the soil needs anything added to it to help the plants grow, and if so, what should be added. Then, you have to choose which veggies you want to grow, and then buy and plant them. Then you'll have to remember to water and care for the plants over time. Because there are several **related tasks** involved in planting your garden, it's a project.

- ❑ **Get a job**—You'll need a resume, and need to figure out what sort of job you want. Then, you'll need to figure out where you're going to send your resume, how and when to follow up, what to wear to the interview, how to answer interview questions. Because what type of resume you need and what you will wear to the interview depends—or is a **dependency**—on what sort of job you are applying for, it's a project!

- ❑ **Plan a trip to Comic-Con**—Let's say you promised yourself a trip to Comic-Con if you managed to get all As in the last school term—and you did! Now, you have to get tickets to the event, figure out when you want to fly there and back, get the airline tickets, and figure out where you are going to stay. Because some of these tasks are **sequential**—it makes no sense to book the flights if you have

---

1   http://en.wikipedia.org/wiki/Project_management. Retrieved May 22, 2014.

not yet gotten the tickets—it's a project.

❑ **Organize your closet**—Your Aunt Violet is coming to visit you from Mississippi in two weeks, and she needs a place to hang her dresses. Unfortunately, your closet is a mess, and you will need to clean and organize it, give away some of the old clothes you've been storing there, and maybe find another place to store a few things—all in two weeks. And, because you are at work all day, you can only work on this in the evening. Because this must be completed by a certain time—or is **time-bound**—it's a project!

You can see that many of the tasks we undertake are actually projects—a set of smaller, interdependent tasks—buy pea plants, throw out old clothes—that all must come together in a certain way in order for us to be successful at the larger goal. And this is precisely where many of us get bogged down, and fail at the overall goal—we have not identified and planned for all the smaller tasks needed, or we get overwhelmed by them before we even begin. Sound familiar?

The trick, then, is to understand some fundamental principles of project management and apply them to your day-to-day life.

Project Management Basics

Before we jump right in, you need to know some of the common terms used in project management—you don't have to become a pro here, but you do need to understand some key components of project management. Here are some common terms:

❑ **Mission Statement**—An overarching principle that drives our 'mindful' actions, such as 'live a happy life' or 'help others by using the talents I have.' Mission statements are common in businesses, but not so much in day-to-day life—and that may be a problem right there. What do we want out of life? How much time and thought do we put into figuring out what we want to do with this life we've been given?

❑ **Goal**—Usually, one of several things that we want to accomplish in our effort to meet some part of our 'Mission Statement', whether to just survive (make enough money to live on) or to fulfill a higher purpose (learn to speak more languages so I can help more people). We can call these 'big projects' in that there are usually several things we must do over a fairly long period of time in order to meet our goal.

❑ **Objective**—A specific sub-set of actions that line up with our goals, such as 'learn Japanese and Spanish' or 'get a higher-paying job.' These are small projects—they are typically of shorter duration than a big project, but also have more than one task needed to complete it. Sometimes we can break down objectives into sub-objectives.

❑ **Tasks**—The actual things we will do to accomplish our objectives toward meeting our goals, such as 'find a Japanese tutor who lives near public transportation.' This is the level where you actually start doing the work, and typically—though not always—involve completing a single 'thing.'

Time for a visual!

In the illustration above, most of us would realize that 'Getting straight As in high school' might take a few more sub-tasks, such as, 'Study every single day for four straight years,' but this gives you an idea of how a long-term goal breaks down into smaller units. And if you don't break it down into these component pieces, getting to your longer-term goal will be next to impossible.

Finally, one more term you absolutely need to know in order to be successful in any project:

❑ **SMART**—a rubric used to 'test' how 'doable' a goal is or is not—Specific, Measurable, Actionable, Realistic, Time-bound.

No matter how well-organized and thought-out a project is, if it does not meet the SMART criteria, it is unlikely to be completed. Simple as that!

Your Own Personal Mission Statement

So, why all this talk about mission statements, goals, tasks and whatnot? Why is it important to go through all of these terms?

The reason it is important is because many people are not familiar with these concepts nor do they realize that there is a **hierarchy** in place between high-level desires (I want to be fabulously wealthy) and the lower-level tasks they might do to be fabulously wealthy (go to a prestigious university and become a famous attorney). Remember these two rules:

> **Rule #1**—If you don't know where you are going, you will never get there. (Your personal mission statement.)

> **Rule #2**—If you don't know *how* you will get there, you probably won't. (The goals, objectives, and tasks needed to accomplish your mission statement.)

Let's start by writing down three mission statements—real ones for yourself, or ones you make up for something/someone else:

Mission Statement 1:
Sample: Attain world domination.

Mission Statement 2:

Mission Statement 3:

Let's look at them—are they overarching principals? Are they too vague (be happy) or too specific (date a supermodel)? How can we rewrite them (find love and build a relationship)? Are they **SMART**?

Once we have nailed a solid mission statement, we can start to identify what goals we have that align with our mission statement. For example, if our mission statement is 'to lead a diva lifestyle,' getting a minimum wage job may not be an appropriate goal, whereas working our butt off to go a prestigious university may be a good goal.

Next, let's talk about what makes a goal/objective/task SMART. Let's say that one of your goals is to earn more money. Is that specific? Is it measurable? Can you do it and is it realistic? Can you do it in a given amount of time? Let's have a look:

Earn More Money
Okay, that's our goal—earn more money. Let's see if it follows the SMART rubric:

- ❏ **Specific?** Yes, but probably not specific enough. Getting a one cent raise is earning more money, but probably won't satisfy the larger mission. Better to state earn $10,000 for example.

- ❏ **Measurable?** Yes, you can measure having earned $10,000 by adding up your pay stubs or looking at your tax returns, but does this mean earning $10,000 overall, or having $40,000 that you've socked away in your savings account? Be certain you know how you plan on measuring it—here, better to say have $10,000 in my savings account. That is definitely measurable!

- ❏ **Actionable?** Can you act on this? Well, if you are going to school full-time and having to watch a younger sibling in all of your off-hours, it may not be actionable in that you don't have the time to work for hire. But for most people, getting a job to earn money is actionable—maybe we should rephrase it as get a job and save up $10,000 in my savings account. That is definitely actionable!

- ❏ **Realistic?** Is this plan so far realistic? Is it a realistic expectation that you could get a job and that you could save up $10,000? Yes! Unless you have some mitigating circumstances, nearly anyone can get a job and save this much money given enough time.

- ❏ **Timebound?** So far, we haven't talked about when this amount of money will be in your savings account, but it's important to nail this down. If we give ourselves too much wiggle room—like, not stating any time frame—we run the risk of not working as hard as we could to accomplish this goal. On the other hand, if we set an unrealistic time frame such as one month, we are sabotaging our chances of success. Time frames must be realistic. Something along the lines of get a job and save up $10,000 in my savings account by June 1st, 20xx. Perfect!

Now, you try this—pick one of the **Mission Statements** you wrote down on the previous page, rewrite it here, and then brainstorm five Goals for that Mission Statement. Remember, goals should 'line up' with an aspect of the higher Mission Statement, but be a bit more specific:

My Mission Statement:
Sample: Attain world domination.

Great, now write down five goals that support your mission statement. Remember, a goal is a set of tasks needed to accomplish your mission. For example, *get a job and save up $10,000 in my savings account by June 1st.*

Goal 1:
Sample: Train all dogs worldwide to defend me through brain control by the end of the millennium.

Goal 2:

Goal 3:

Goal 4:

Goal 5:

Great, now check each one and see if they are SMART...do you need to rewrite any of them? If so, do so now.

Moving on now to **Objectives**—pick one of the above goals, and write out the objectives for that goal—remember, it should be more specific than the goal itself—if the goal was get a job and save up $10,000 in my savings account by June 1st, what is a specific, actionable objective toward that goal? A few objectives that support this goal include *get a job, cancel my Gamefly subscription to save money* and *investigate savings accounts with the highest yield.*

Now, you try—write at least two objectives that support one of your goals above, more if you can:

Objective 1:
Sample: Develop method to control the world's dogs by December 31st.

Objective 2:

Objective 3:

Objective 4:

Objective 5:

Once again, have a look to see if these objectives are SMART—and again rewrite them if needed.

Finally, we get to the actual tasks! This is where you actually start doing the work needed to meet your objectives, goals, and overall mission statement. Pick one of your objectives from above, and write down the **tasks** that you might need to do to meet that objective. For example, if one of your objectives was to get a job, appropriate tasks might include update my resume, apply for part time jobs, go to networking events. Write at least three, and up to five objectives, and don't forget to check to make sure they are SMART!

Task 1:
Sample: Hire mad scientist from Craigslist to develop radio-controlled, lithium battery powered dog collars that emit high frequency sounds not audible by humans by June 1st.

Task 2:

Task 3:

Task 4:

Task 5:

This starts looking an awful lot like a To-Do list, doesn't it? Well, it is—but instead of just random things that need to be done, these tasks support a goal. And this is how we make larger things happen in our lives—by articulating what it is we want out of life and understanding the ways we can get there. Project management isn't just for projects—we can use these skills to accomplish any type of goal.

Committing to Your Goals

You may have heard the saying that someone is afraid of "The 'C' word," meaning that they are afraid of commitment, or specifically committing to a course of action, such as a long-term relationship.

While we may joke about men being afraid to 'commit' to a relationship with someone, what most of us don't realize is that we are all often afraid to commit to change. Creating a life mission statement and actually working on it actively is a form of commitment, and in a very real way, it is a relationship—a relationship with change and how we would like to live our lives.

Most of us will not be able to accomplish everything we would like to do in our lives—there is simply too much to do, and not enough time to do it. So, we have to select the things that are the most important to us—to things like the way we want to live our lives, how we perceive ourselves, and want others to remember us for when we are gone. Heady stuff, eh? No wonder we are afraid to commit! These are big decisions!

But, in the end, doing something is frequently better than doing nothing—as the Taoist saying goes, the journey of a thousand miles starts with a single step. It's time to take that step! Go back to your Goals section, and pick one of the goals you would like to work on, then write it down, and answer the following questions:

My Goal (remember, make it SMART):

❑ **I want to do this because:**

❑ **I think I can do this because:**

❑ **I believe I am ready to do this because:**

Now, finally, write down all of the tasks that will be needed to accomplish this goal.

Task 1:

Task 2:

Task 3:

Task 4:

Task 5:

If a given task is too big to work on directly, you may need to break down that task further. We will talk about the finer points of project management in the next section.

Using What You Know to Succeed

So far in this book, you've learned several tricks to help you overcome some very common executive functioning barriers—ways to better manage your time by using calendars and alarms to keep you on task, ways to organize your physical and virtual worlds to help you process information more effectively, ways to study and learn in more coherent ways. And now, how to break down a big idea or project into smaller chunks so that you have a good shot at getting where you want to be.

So now, take a few minutes to review your mission statement, goals, and tasks, and flip back to the end pages of previous chapters—what have you learned about yourself, how you work, what gets in your way? How might those things help or hinder you now? Jot down what you now know as it pertains to working on the project you have written down here.

Goal Commitment—Don't Give Up!

We'll talk about why people give up in later chapters, but for now, know this—most of us have failed, sometimes many times, before we succeeded. Case in point—my original goal was to have this book to the publisher 24 months ago. I have been working on this book for well over four years, and some days I thought I'd never finish it. It would be easy to give up. Nothing bad would happen, and it's unlikely that I will be rewarded with fame and fortune if I finish it (as wonderful as that might be!).

What got me through this was a situation—a dear friend coming to stay with us, who wanted to help me with something in return. And, she just happens to be an excellent writer. I knew this was my opportunity to have her help me finish the book. I might be able to do it alone, but it would take me longer, to be sure. The situation presented itself, and I seized the opportunity to use it to both of our benefits—hers, to find a way to do something for me while she found a new apartment in the area, and mine to have her come stay with us while she did that.

We both had something the other needed. We both helped the other with our personal struggles with commitment to follow through. How can you make that work for yourself?

ThoughtBox: Help for Commitment Phobia

In his book *Carrots and Sticks* (2010), Ian Ayres talks about different methods to get people to commit to change, and discusses why so many of us are phobic and resist doing the things we know would benefit us. Ayres describes several ways we can set ourselves up for success by using commitment techniques.

We have all heard of arrangements where a parent will pay a student to get better grades, and many companies incent their workers to produce more by offering them the possibility of bonuses. These financial commitments tend to work when money is a 'desired object,' but what about when a person has no real desire for extra cash (and yes, such people exist), or not enough desire to make the change?

Ayres suggests an alternate method whereby non-compliance results in the non-compliant 'changee' paying for his/her failure—literally. Imagine setting up a commitment system, where you agreed to give $100 to a friend to hold for you, and if you failed in your commitment, this friend would give your money to an organization that is the antithesis of what you cared about—so that if you were a devout Catholic you could pledge money to a satanic cult if you spent more than your allotted time on the internet, or if you were a liberal pacifist trying to exercise three times a week, you could pledge to make a donation to the NRA if you missed a day. Would that motivate you?

We could certainly come up with some compelling pledging strategies here (smokers donating to the tobacco lobbyists, internet addicts sending a check to Mark Zuckerberg, compulsive gamers packing up their Xboxes and mailing them to the dump—in another state), and while these are great ways to incent people to follow through on a commitment, some people will still resist, or not make good on their pledge, which may further cause them to resist any change – See? I can't do it, no matter what. How would you handle that?

As Ayres suggests, you plan "for the possibility of failure [so that you] can increase the probability of success."[1] What Ayres is referring to here is a reset, or in more common parlance, a do-over – understanding in advance that we

---

1   Ayres, I. (2010). *Carrots and Sticks: Unlock the power of incentives to get things done.* Bantam Books, New York, NY, pp. 28.

may fail at our first—or second, or third—attempt, and building that into our commitment strategy. How could you make this strategy work for you? Is there anything you feel passionate enough about that you would do anything to protect?

Some people's behaviors are so entrenched that they require more odious methods. Disabling commitments, which Ayres calls "hand-tying arrangements,"[2] are designed to "take the choice off the table" by removing access or making use exceedingly unpleasant. Two well-known drugs, Antabuse and alli, are effective disabling commitment strategies, make drinking alcohol or overeating (respectively) physically unpleasant. Another type of disabling commitment would be applications such as Cybersitter or NetNanny which disallow access to specific internet sites, or the internet as a whole at specific times of day. While these tools may seem draconian, if you are really struggling to make a change, you may need big guns.

Another form of commitment strategies comes from the book *Reality is Broken: Why Games Make Us Better and How They Can Change the World* (2011) by Jane McGonigal, a noted game designer. While McGonigal acknowledges that internet use can become problematic, she suggests, essentially, if you can't beat 'em, join 'em—make life more like a game! And she has a point. Gaming is highly addictive in large part because we get near-immediate feedback on our performance, and when we do well, we get an intense rush—what she refers to as a *fiero* moment. How far can you take gaming? How about a role-playing website dedicated to chores, where your roommates or family members create characters and vie for points by emptying the dishwasher? Check out *Chore Wars* (www.chorewars.com) where you can do just that.

What all of these examples suggest is that one sure-fire way to succeed is to engage with others to help us succeed. Set it up so that others we care about are dependent on our success. Set it up so that something relatively bad will happen if we fail. Set it up so that it is a game to do things we see as chores. McGonigal rightly calls this "the self-help paradox."[3] When commitment is scarce, we need outside forces to compel us into the behavior we want to see in ourselves.

2   Ibid., pp. 66.
3   McGonigal, J. (2011). *Reality is broken: Why games make us better and how they can change the world*. The Penguin Press, New York, NY, pp. 186.

Your Project Management Profile

As you've seen, project management is really identifying your goals, detailing how you will accomplish your goals—and if you're stuck, making sure you know how to get others to follow through on what you want to do. Make it work for you!

My Mission Statement

Goals In Support of My Mission	
1.	
2.	
3.	

Tasks In Support of My Goals		
Goal 1	1.	
	2.	
	3.	
Goal 2	1.	
	2.	
	3.	
Goal 3	1.	
	2.	
	3.	

Where Can I Get Help or Motivation?

Information Management

How we think, plan, and make decisions are basic forms of information management. We know that our brains like to take random things and make order out of them, and that this helps us remember things, helps us accomplish what we set out to do, and generally keeps us—and our lives—running efficiently.

We all use common tools to process information, but most of us are unaware that we do so, and do not use these processing tools consciously most of the time. But, when used appropriately, these 'algorithms' can help us make better decisions, look out for possible problems in the future, understand why things are not working, and other important pieces of information. Let's have a look.

Sorting Information

As we've discussed in the first part of this book, our brain is constantly sorting the information it receives from our five senses, and sorts this information in a variety of ways. One of the first criteria our brains use to determine what to do with sensory input is based on importance to self—do I need to pay attention to this information for my safety (smell of smoke), for my enjoyment (someone I like is calling my name), for my well-being (following instructions from a teacher), for my health (feeling hungry) and so forth.

If our brains were not able to sort and filter information this way, we would go stark raving mad—we simply take in too much information for us to respond to all at once. Sounds, smells, sights, tactile feelings, tastes—our limbic system would be inundated by reactions—to the sound of the faucet dripping, the way our shirt tag felt, the tiny itch on our foot, the reflected light on our computer screen. Only a small portion of what our brains take in from the environment is passed to our conscious minds to react on or to.

And, as we discussed earlier in this book, many people who have sensory issues have a difficult time not responding to information in their environment, or difficulty responding appropriately—we call this '*sensory overload*' for a very good reason, though it's not our senses—but the 'filters' in our brains—that are overloaded. Additionally, some people may in fact be filtering out too much information, and the brain 'gets sleepy' without enough arousal to keep it focused on necessary tasks. This is why some folks with ADHD need to listen to music when they read, chew gum, tap their fingers, or take medication—they need additional sensory stimulation to stay focused.

So, how does your brain sort or filter? Do you think you filter out too much or too little sensory input, or just about the right amount of information? If too little or too much, what do you do—or could you do—to compensate? Write down your thoughts below.

Now, let's talk about that small portion of sensory input that gets passed to your conscious mind—what do you do with that information? If typical, you still can't react to everything all at once all the time. That would be exhausting and non-productive. We need more tools to make 'sense' of this information! And guess what—we do have tools! Tools that can sort incoming information by:

- ❑ Relatedness
- ❑ Importance
- ❑ Validity

Relatedness

Sorting by relatedness simply means—is this information related to something I have already determined is important? If I am making dinner, and the timer for the oven goes off at the same time as the dryer stops, sorting by relatedness would say—go to the oven, not the dryer—the dry clothes can wait a bit while I finish dinner, because it is not part of the overall goal at hand (make dinner). In other words, does this information need to be acted upon to meet my higher level, already established goal of making dinner? This may seem simple, but the fact of the matter is, we frequently get distracted by non-related activities when we are working on a goal. How does responding to an IM on Facebook help us get homework done? Ahem, it doesn't!

Here's a little exercise to try. Match the 'sensory input' or thought with the overall goal by drawing a line to it.

Sensory Input/Thoughts	Overall Goal
I smell smoke from the oven	
I really want to read that book	Relax
I wonder if we have rice, I should check	
Phone is ringing	
Where is the shampoo	
The oil in the pan is hot	
I wonder what is on TV	
The dog is happier when I give him a cookie	Make Dinner
The rice cooker just went off with a click	
The dog is whimpering	
I'd really like a nap, I'm sleepy	
There are vegetables in the sink	
I have to find the dog brush	Wash the Dog
Someone IMed me on Facebook	
All the forks are dirty	
The dog is wet, and I need towels	

As you can see, some thoughts are 'valid' for the task at hand. For example, it's reasonable to check to see if there is rice if the goal you are working on is '*making dinner.*' If the goal at hand, however, is '*wash the dog*', thinking about rice isn't very helpful. This isn't to say that we should never allow an 'invalid' thought to creep in—if we are washing the dog and we smell smoke from the oven, we need to respond to that input for our safety.

It's important to note here that thoughts or interruptions such as an IM chime or a ringing telephone are optional—this is something many people have a difficult time wrapping their heads around because our limbic systems want us to react (hear a bell, respond). But we can (and frequently should) ignore these interruptions when we are trying to complete a task. We can always call back, or check our messages when we have finished our work.

Importance

Sorting by importance is another way to sort information, and while useful most of the time, we get caught up in many activities that appear to our limbic system to be important, but which actually distract us from what we are trying to do. Can you list three things that feel important but that distract you from your work sometimes?

1.

2.

3.

What is it about these items that make them feel important, when in fact they really are not? Generally speaking, it's because they are **time-bound**—they feel important because they are *happening right now*—the phone is ringing, your friend is waiting for you to IM back, the floor needs vacuuming and your friend will be here any minute (okay, the last is a stretch, but still!). They feel important because they are urgent—but the question is, are they really important? We all get caught up in this very easily—and here are the things that appear important (because they are urgent) but that absolutely kill our productivity and focus:

- ❑ Email
- ❑ IM
- ❑ Text
- ❑ Phone
- ❑ Door bell
- ❑ Interactive/online gaming
- ❑ Housework/chores/errands

Not one of these is usually important enough to respond to right away, if it means that we will lose our focus on a goal we must complete. This does not mean that you have to be hyper-focused and never distracted, but it does mean that you should consciously choose whether or not to be distracted by the information your brain is receiving. Think when the phone is ringing—do I need to answer that, or can I listen to a message later?

If you cannot shut out the distraction by telling your mind to stop responding, then you need to remove the distraction altogether. Shut down your email application. Quit out of your IM accounts. Turn your phone off. Quit out of your internet browser. *Remove the temptation!*

Validity

Validity is another way we sort information that comes in to our brain. Similar to Importance in the preceding section, our brains pass through information to us that may not be valid—the sensory input is accurate, but the response that our brain comes up with is not. Take a look at these examples—and circle the most VALID explanation.

Sensory Input/Thoughts	Possible Thoughts
My phone just chimed twice—I have two new text messages.	If it were important, they'd call. I'll check them after the meeting.
	Clearly, this is an emergency! I have to look now!
I heard a pretty big thud outside.	I know I'm supposed to be working on my paper, but that sounded dangerous. I'll go check!
	It's probably Mr. Hedges working in his garage.
That woman looked at me strangely.	I probably look familiar.
	Ack! I must have done something wrong! I better leave right away!

Validity is a way of identifying whether or not we are 'fooling' ourselves into a **distraction action**, or undertaking something that we really do not need to do—something that is not helping us in the path to our goals. We are all very good at this type of thing, and those who are also easily distracted, worried, fearful, or eager to please those around us are spectacular at this type of distracted thinking.

The best way to determine if something is valid is to ask the question: *What will happen—really—if I don't do this right now?* If there is truly a dire consequence—truly—then, it may be valid to do it now.

Ranking Information

Ranking information is another way to find out what is truly important—in relation to other information/items on your list of things to do. This is a really useful tool when everything needs to be done (or feels like it needs to be done) and you are completely overwhelmed by the length of the list.

In business, this is sometimes called **stacked ranking** and it simply means going through all of the items on your list and trying to ascertain what is *the* most important item on the list—the one thing that you must do in order to achieve your goal.

For example, let's say that your overall goal is to have more money. All of the items below are ways to either make more money or save money, but they are not all equal in their effectiveness in getting money into your pocket.

Go through this list, and determine what you think is number 1 in importance to this goal, number 2, and so forth, in each category (Impact, Urgency, Most effective). What will have the highest impact on getting more money into your bank account?

Action Item	Impact (big change)	Urgency (how fast)	Most Effective (long term)
Stop eating at McDonald's for lunch every day			
Cancel cable stations I don't watch much			
Get a higher-paying job			
Sell all my old CDs on Amazon.com (about 50)			
Stop buying my girlfriend a book for her birthday each year			
Buy groceries at Trader Joe's rather than at 7-11			

Evaluating Information

Once we have stacked ranked our information, we still need to do some more evaluation, or we may miss an important piece of information, depending on the situation.

For example, let's say that you must come up with $200 in two weeks or lose out on a great opportunity. Getting a new job will have the highest impact, but can you get a new job and earn $200 in two weeks? Probably not. So, getting a job in this situation would be most effective in the long term, but not very good at getting cash quickly. Selling your CDs, however, may get you some of the cash you need right away.

Let's say the Mafia isn't after you, and you have some time to get more money— the next way to evaluate your options is by how efficient, over time, each item is to generate income or reduce expenses. So, take the time to go back and rank these items again based on how effective over time each one would be. Getting a job and saving money by shopping at Trader Joe's would probably be good solutions.

See how you come up with different answers each time? Your specific situation will provide key information you need when you are making decisions. Think deeply and clearly about all of the possibilities and how effective they will be in attaining your overall goal.

Finally, there are two other ways to evaluate information—using **Pros and Cons**, and **low-hanging fruit** vs. **stretch goals**.

Let's do Pros and Cons first, using the same information as before. Using the list on the following page, and with the same goal of having more money, what are the positives (pros) and negatives (cons) of each possible item?

As you can probably see by filling in the chart on the following page, there are some unwanted consequences of taking a few of these actions. If you sell your CDs, you won't have music to listen to (unless you upload them to iTunes first!). If you stop buying your girlfriend a birthday present, she probably won't be your girlfriend for long. It's important to check your intended solutions this way to make sure that they don't end up biting you in the proverbial butt!

Action Item	Pros	Cons
Stop eating at McDonald's for lunch every day		
Cancel cable stations I don't watch much		
Get a higher-paying job		
Sell all my old CDs on Amazon.com (about 50)		
Stop buying my girlfriend a book for her birthday each year		
Buy groceries at Trader Joe's rather than at 7-11		

Yet another way to evaluate solutions is by determining how easy or hard each item might be to do. Easy solutions are called **Low-hanging Fruit**—easy to reach. Hard solutions—ones that might be hard to do, or take a while to accomplish—are called **Stretch Goals**.

Go through the list above one more time, and identify with a check mark those items which would be easiest to do, and which one of these items might be hard to do.

ThoughtBox: All Trees, No Forest

One of the things that many of our clients struggle with is identifying what is important information, and what is not. This is '*all trees, no forest*'—a bunch of seemingly unrelated items with no binding theme. This is especially troublesome when taking notes, when writing papers, when preparing a speech, or when developing a brief for work. What is the salient information you need to collect, understand, or convey? Some keys to identifying important information when reading include:

❑ **What is the main point?** This is very different in fiction, where the point or the theme may take a while to recognize, and nonfiction, where the point is to impart information on a given topic. When reading non-fiction, a textbook for example, pay attention to 'informational road signs' such as the title of the book (*History of the Middle Ages*), the chapter (*Roman Influences*) and headings (*Aqueducts*). These will help you identify which 'trees' or details to pay attention to.

❑ **Who, What, Where, How, and When**. Once you can identify the main topic of a section, the next salient information to note is the facts – the whos, whats, wheres, whys, whens, and hows, and so forth. Who built the aqueducts, how, where, and when?

❑ **Synthesize the Information.** As you read along, it is very useful to stop occasionally, and write down what you have learned. This can be a simple task, where for each section read, you create a sheet with the chapter and section title (Roman Influences/Aqueducts) and a list of who, what, where, and so forth. Finally, write one or two sentences summarizing the section.

❑ **'Pre-Read' the Material.** If you're having difficulty with a particular subject, see if there is a chapter overview or summary. If so, read the summary first—this is what the author wants you to take away from the chapter. Then read the overview—this is what the author intends to teach you. Write down the points in the overview. Now, with this information in mind—the key take-away points, and the teaching objectives, read the chapter. You have already loaded up your pre-conscious mind with what you are looking for, and your brain is primed for learning. Go forth!

ThoughtBox: All Trees, No Forest, *Continued*

You can use this same method when listening to lectures. Read any supporting information ahead of time, write down what you think the lecturer is trying to teach you, then take notes focusing on those items. If at all possible, ask for a copy of the presentation ahead of time. It really is that easy, and gets easier with practice. We frequently ask for advance notes or presentations as part of accommodations in school for students with learning disabilities.

When you are developing material for others, be it a presentation, a paper, or a speech, start with the end in mind. *What do you want to tell your audience?* That is your thesis statement. *What is the supporting evidence to this thesis?* Tell them that next. Finally, reiterate what you have demonstrated. As one teacher told me in college – 1. Tell them what you're going to tell them. 2. Tell them. 3. Tell them what you told them! That's it!

Considering Resources

We've looked at several different ways of sorting and evaluating information based on different factors—quick results, long-term results, easy to do, harder to do, and we've talked about watching out for unwanted consequences—those things that we can look ahead and avoid (like, our girlfriend getting mad at us because we did not buy her a gift!).

There is one more—and very important—factor you must consider when making decisions—what resources will you need, and when? There are three types of resources that impact decisions: time, money, and scope, or how much needs to be done. The theory is that if you skimp on any of the three resources, you will impact the quality of the job you are trying to do.

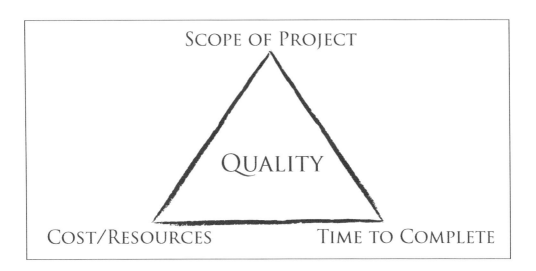

Needed Resources

So, let's do a quick run-through. Let's say you have 50 pages of a book you must read and take notes on before a test on Friday at 8 am. It is now Wednesday evening at 8 pm.

- ❏ **Scope**—50 pages plus written notes
- ❏ **Cost/Resources**—you (no one else can do this for you!)
- ❏ **Time to Complete**—36 hours

Okay, now let's figure that you can read 20 pages an hour if you read non-stop. So, it would take 2.5 hours of your time to complete this task. If you are going to do a quality job on this project, you will need to find 2.5 hours in the next 36 hours to do this reading. If you do not spend this much time reading, you have changed the scope, and your quality—your grade on the test—will go down. If you start but do not finish the reading, you have changed the resources (your time) and again, your grade on the test will go down!

Many things you do in life do not require a lot of thought about resources—you simply do them when you can. However, as your life becomes more complex and your available time becomes shorter, thinking about your own resources is very important. If you are going to school full-time and working a part-time job, you will need to set aside time to do your homework. Your resource in this case is your time.

Money is another resource to consider. If you have been saving up to buy a car, but you unexpectedly had to purchase a new printer for school, you have less money for the car. Your choices are to buy a less expensive car, which will impact the quality of the car, or to save your money for a longer time, which increases the time to complete.

Sequencing and Dependencies

Other aspects to consider when planning a project are **sequencing** and **dependencies**. Sequencing is being mindful of which steps have to be done in which order—for example, you can't write up the notes for your homework if you have not done the reading yet. These must be done in sequence—read, then take notes.

Dependencies are often related to sequencing—figuring out what items you have to do first, and in what order, if necessary. Writing the notes is dependent on reading the book. Sometimes dependencies are related to other resources. For example, if forgot to bring home your book from school, a dependency on doing your homework may be on whether or not you can borrow the text from a friend.

Hours vs. Duration

Another concept that is important when thinking about projects and how we get things done are hours vs. duration.

Hours refers to the actual number of hours we estimate a particular task to take to complete. This should be a realistic number. So for example, if the task is to go to the library and research three philosophers, 30 minutes is not an accurate estimate. Why? Because unless you live right next to the library, it will take you at least a few minutes to get there and back—so you need to figure that in, too.

A general rule of thumb in business is the 'time and a half' rule—meaning simply that if you think something is going to take you 60 minutes to accomplish, give yourself 90 minutes. This additional time, called **slack**, gives you a nice cushion in case something takes longer than expected. And, something nearly always takes longer than expected. If not, that's great—you bought yourself some free time!

Duration, on the other hand, refers to the time span—in days, weeks, or months—it will take us to finish a task. Again, the point here is to be realistic. There are 24 hours in a day, eight of which we are asleep, more or less. We may be in school, working a job, eating dinner, driving around, etc., meaning that the actual time we have to work on any project on a given day is quite limited.

So, my dear friends, you will not be able to finish a 20-page paper on *Life During the Depression* in one day, unless you don't do anything else. And, if you try to do it in one day, it will likely be crap. Ahem. Here's an example:

Go to Library	2 hours	day 1
Start outline	1 hour	day 1
Finish outline	1 hour	day 2
Write topic paragraph	.5 hours	day 2
Interview Gramma	.5 hours	day 2

When you write down the duration, you are in effect committing that much time on that day—here, we've committed 3 hours of work on Day 1, and 2 hours of work on Day 2. Again, *be realistic*! If you load yourself up with too much work, and then start to fall behind, you will lose steam, the project will fall apart, and you will give up. Slow and steady, slow and steady. Think *Tortoise*, not *Hare*!

ThoughtBox: All Forest, No Trees

Another problem some people have is being so overwhelmed by data that they literally cannot identify any one thing to focus on when asked a question – every piece of information vies for attention. This happens a great deal with 'sensory overloaded' individuals, such as those with ADHD, ASD, learning challenges and synesthesia (a miswiring of one or more of the senses, where a person 'hears' colors, or 'sees' music for example).

This virtual flood of information makes it difficult to sort information into manageable chunks or groups. I call it the 'black box syndrome' where everything seems to be fused together into one whole. So, if asked, for example, *What is in your bedroom*, the individual cannot answer. Too many things immediately came to mind, all crowding into consciousness, and the individual cannot pick one thing – it is all forest, no trees. Everything in this individual's room seems 'glued' together.

ThoughtBox: All Forest, No Trees, *Continued*

In cases like these, we need to break down the big group (the forest) by identifying common subset elements—here, a way for the individual to 'sort' the contents of her room, so that she can identify the individual components (the trees). We can create these general buckets:

- ❑ **Furniture** – I have a bed, a desk, and two bookshelves.
- ❑ **Floor coverings** – Nothing, I have a hardwood floor.
- ❑ **Lighting** – I have a lamp on my desk, and a light on the ceiling.

This system is very useful when you have a lot of information to sort through, and need a way to identify logical groupings into which you will place an individual idea or item. With career clients, I create bottom-up classification systems all the time. After they have done assessment and their career exploration, they deliver to me a list of all the jobs that sound interesting to them (a bunch of unrelated trees). We then write them on the white board, and I sort them into groupings:

Job	Job Family	Education Needed	Income
Vet tech	Animal jobs	AA	$
Zoologist		BA+	$$$
(Park naturalist)		BA+	$$
Food scientist	Lab jobs	BA+	$$
Microbiologist		MA+	$$$
Biochem tech		AA	$
Teacher	Helping/Teaching	MA+	$$
Therapist		MA+	$$$
(Park naturalist)		BA+	$$

Sorting or creating a **taxonomy** such as above makes it much easier to use information and make decisions, and to see connections between data. How can you use this type of sorting when you have too much information?

Your Turn!

Let's see how you can apply these concepts to an actual project. Pick a project you need to work on (it could be clean out the garage, write a paper, get a job, whatever), list the individual steps needed to complete the project, and then realistically estimate how many days it will take to do each item in the chart below. If you can get more than one item done, just write down the same number on those lines, as we described earlier.

Project Name:

TASK		HOURS	DURATION
1.			
2.			
3.			
4.			
5.			
6.			
7.			
8.			
9.			
10.			
11.			
12.			
13.			
14.			

Sequencing

Once you have all of your tasks down in the list above, the next step is to check to make sure all items are in the proper sequence, and if not, to reorder them. So, go back through your list above and write down a number (1, 2, 3. etc) next to those items that must be done in sequence. Leave out any items that do not have to be done in a specific order—we'll deal with those in the next step. Think about the natural flow of things, and try to envision what would be first, second, and so forth.

Non-Dependent Tasks

Now go back and **circle** the items that can be done at any time or in any sequence. You don't need to do anything else with them right now; just make them stand out a bit.

Dependencies

Dependencies can be a bit trickier, because they may be situation-specific. For example, I have a laser printer in my office, so printing my work does not have any dependencies on it other than finishing the task. For someone who does not have a printer, this would be a dependency—buy and install the printer before printing the document!

Remember, dependencies basically fall into two categories: **sequencing dependencies** (which we have already identified above) and **resource dependences** (I can't do this until I have access to that resource). For example, if I'm interviewing my mother and she is out of town for two weeks, I have a resource dependency. If I need to go to the library but can't over the weekend because it is closed, I have both a sequencing and a resource dependency—I can't write the paper until the library is open, and the library won't be open until next week.

Go back over your list, and see if there are any non-sequencing (meaning, resource) dependencies—if so, mark them with an **R** for resource. Great!!

Resource List

Now, **copy the items from your list** that you identified as needed Resources below. Also identify any other resources you need to complete your project—help from a friend, lumber from the home improvement store, printer cartridges or paper, and so forth.

Our Final (sort of) Task List

Now that we have written out our tasks, ordered them, and determined all of our dependencies, we can rewrite them into a nice, neat list. Do that below:

TASKS   **HOURS**   **DURATION**

1._____   _____

2._____   _____

3._____   _____

4._____   _____

5._____   _____

6._____   _____

7._____   _____

8._____   _____

9._____   _____

10._____   _____

11._____   _____

12._____   _____

13._____   _____

14._____   _____

15._____   _____

16._____   _____

Great. Once you have your task list done, go back, and write in your best estimate of hours each task will take, then write in the duration for each task. Add up the numbers—both of hours and days/weeks it will take to complete this goal.

After you have written in the hours and duration, highlight any items with **yellow** that are **not** dependent, either by sequence or resource, to other items. These are the items we will 'fit in' when you have a spare moment, if there are any dependency gaps.

Finally, write down what **date** you want to start working on your goal. Can you start right away, or are there things you need to do? If possible, your start date should be within the next two weeks.

Staying (or Getting Back) On Track

Now that you have identified a project, thought it through, figured out what sequence tasks should be completed, what resources you need, and so forth, the project should just glide through to completion without a hitch, right? Maybe, if you live on a different planet than I live on!

The truth of the matter is that no matter how well we plan, things do come up. For example, we have to work on another project, we come down with a cold, or we simply get distracted. And once we have fallen even a day behind our schedule, the temptation is great to just stop pushing forward. We have been struck by entropy—a body in motion tends to stay in motion and a body at rest—well, tends to stay on the couch playing Halo.

This does not mean failure. What it means is that life has intervened, and you will now have to steel yourself to start again. Depending on how long you got off track, this may just mean you have to work twice as hard on a given day to catch up. Or, if you have really been waylaid, it may make sense to quickly go through and recalculate the dates until completion. You don't have to redo the whole plan, because the only thing that has changed is the date—we call this slipping, when the original end date slips out by a few days, weeks, or sometimes even months. It happens. And if you had already built in a bit of slack into your schedule, then the world is not over. Just take a deep breath, and start where you left off.

If you are really having a difficult time staying on track, you may want to add some additional structure to the project in the form of oversight. What this simply means is asking someone to meet with you on a regular basis to make sure that you are indeed staying on schedule. This person could be a parent or a friend, a mentor or instructor, or a life coach—someone who is sympathetic to the fact that this is a hard skill you are learning, but who will find ways to keep you motivated.

You can also think about putting motivators in place on your own. What motivates people? In the work world, we know that while people expect to be paid for their work, this is not really what motivates them. Instead, they respond to praise, perks, and status. So, you don't have to pay yourself when you meet a deadline—instead, why not do something nice for yourself? Maybe buy a new video game you've been wanting to get, or allow yourself to spend an entire day vegging on the couch binge-watching Dr. Who—whatever gives you the sense of reward for a job well done!

If you find that you repeatedly get behind and cannot get back on track, then it may indeed be time to consider working with a life or executive functioning coach to help you. Most of us do much better when someone is 'watching' us. We are almost always more motivated to succeed when we know we will have to explain to someone else why we did not. Coaching is a great way to do this.

Just remember that many people have had to start, restart, and start a project again before it gets finished. It is not uncommon to be interrupted or to get off track. What makes people successful is not that they never get off track—it's their ability to suck it up, and get back on track!

Your Information Management Profile

We've gone through a lot of concepts and terms in this chapter, covering more background on project management concepts around how to break down information into more meaningful chunks, and then how to use that information in support of a larger goal. Now, take the time to go back through this chapter, and make some notes about how you can use these concepts:

My Mission Statement (from *Project Management*)

Resources I Will Need:
1.
2.
3.
4.
5.
6.

Dependencies/Sequencing I Need To Be Aware Of:
1.
2.
3.
4.
5.
6.

Thought Management

Much like managing information, it may seem a bit odd to 'manage' your thoughts. And yet, most of us do exactly this each and every day. In fact, we may have to manage our thoughts—a recent Harvard study shows that we daydream about 50% of our waking hours, and so if we are to get anything done, we will need to manage ourselves.

We do it when we make a conscious attempt to focus on what a speaker is saying, in a meeting or in a class. We do this when we force ourselves to think 'happy thoughts' when someone mentions something disturbing. We do this when we are actively problem-solving, going through a mental list of possible solutions, tossing out the silly and impractical ones, and hanging on to the useful ones.

Thought management, then, has a few different variants:

❑ **Thought Screening**—We screen our thoughts when we need to focus on something, and other thoughts 'pop up,' that intrude on our ability to focus on the task at hand. The thoughts that 'pop up' are generally harmless in and of themselves, but are distracting. We typically manage these thoughts by telling ourselves 'focus!', or 'think about that later,' in an effort to snap out of our previous thoughts.

❑ **Thought Cessation**—Making our thoughts stop or change is another way we 'manage' our thoughts. We may do this after watching a scary movie, or seeing something that disturbs us, by telling ourselves to 'go to our happy place,' but we can also use this type of management when depression or anxiety takes hold of our thoughts and we consciously make an attempt to stop maladaptive or distorted thinking and 'force' ourselves to think more positively or constructively about our current situation.

- ❑ **Thought Sorting**—Thought sorting is a bit like screening, in that we are choosing which thoughts to focus on. We do this when we are problem solving, free associating, and brainstorming—when we are consciously trying to let our brain come up with solutions, and on the fly deciding which thoughts have merit, and which ones to throw out. Thought sorting is very useful in many endeavors such as creative writing.

- ❑ **Thought Running**—A little like thought sorting, thought running is when we take a promising thought or solution, and 'run it' to its most likely conclusion: if we do A, then B is likely to happen, which means C and D will come next. Thought running is very important when making decisions to determine a given decision's most likely outcome.

There are other types of thought management, of course, but these are probably the most useful types on a day to day basis. List some ideas of how and when you can use each of these types of thought management in your day-to-day life:

Thought Screening	1.
	2.
	3.
	4.
Thought Cessation	1.
	2.
	3.
	4.
Thought Sorting	1.
	2.
	3.
	4.
Thought Running	1.
	2.
	3.
	4.

ThoughtBox: The Importance of Mindfulness

One of the things that we are learning here is how to be 'mindful' about what our thoughts are, and how they impact our day-to-day life. But before you can understand how your thoughts can control you, you have to be mindful of what your thoughts are!

It sounds pretty simple, and it actually is—once you realize that all you need to do is learn to check in with yourself on a regular basis to see where your thoughts are. You can do this at regular intervals throughout the day, by doing journaling about your thoughts at the end of each day, by meditating one or more times a day, or in a host of other ways. The important thing to do is to be mindful of our thoughts and how they influence our mood and actions.

List a few ways that you could become more mindful of your thoughts:

1.

2.

3.

4.

5.

Great—now write down five things that might get in your way to becoming more mindful of your thoughts:

1.

2.

3.

4.

5.

Distorted Thinking

Many of us suffer bouts of what Aaron Beck, a distinguished psychiatrist and founder of Cognitive Therapy, described as **distorted thinking**—thinking that serves us in the short term by allowing us to, frankly, make excuses for our mood, behavior or for giving up. Note that we ALL do this from time to time—how frequently depends on the person and how resilient they are. David Burns, another psychiatrist out of Stanford University, described fifteen different types of distorted thinking in his book *Feeling Good: The New Mood Therapy,*[1] which are described below. Again, it's important to remember that all of us use many forms of distorted thinking from time to time—the trick is to catch ourselves doing it.

Read through each type of distorted thinking, along with the example, and on the line underneath each description, write down an instance where you have used this type of distortion in the past, and what you might be able to do to 'rethink' the situation in a more realistic and positive way.

1. **Filtering**—This is about taking a small negative detail, and focusing exclusively, or nearly so, on that one detail, rather than focusing on the many good things about a situation, person, or thing. **Making a mountain out of a molehill** is a phrase used to describe this type of thinking.

    Example: The entire party was completely ruined by the fact that my mother forgot to buy the cheese balls that she knows I love. How could she do that?

    Your example:

2. **Polarized Thinking**— This is where everything is either good or bad, black or white, right or wrong—there is never anything in between, when in fact, many of life's questions can best be answered by 'it depends.' The biggest danger with this type of thinking is when you are thinking about yourself—that if you are not perfect in every way, that you are a failure. This is sometimes called **black or white thinking.**

    Example: I didn't get the part I wanted in the play. I am a complete failure.

    Your example:

---

1   Burns, D. (1980). *Feeling Good: The New Mood Therapy.* HarperCollins, New York, NY.

3. **Overgeneralization**—This is where you state that a generalized outcome based on a single, or small handful, of incidents. Clues that you are overgeneralizing is by using the words **always** and **never**. This distortion can lead to a restricted life, as you avoid future failures based on the single incident or event.

Example: I am never going to a party again. Not one person talked to me the entire time. This always happens.

Your example:

4. **Mind Reading**—Mind reading is when we assume we know how another person feels without their actually telling us how they feel. This is also called **projection**, as we are projecting our thoughts onto someone else. Another form of mind reading is when you assume that other people feel as you do, and will react as you do—that there is no difference in how you think and feel and how others might think and feel. Jumping to conclusions is a phrase that pretty well defines mind reading.

Example: It's absolutely clear that she doesn't like me anymore. She called me four days in a row, and today, nothing. Crickets. She must hate me.

Your example:

5. **Catastrophizing**—While everyone should be prepared for true disasters, people experiencing catastrophized thinking are expecting disaster at every turn, and everything is preceded by a **What if?** Scenario, spelling ultimate ruin. Often times it helps to think in terms of probability and possibility—while it is possible that you could get hit by a crashing airplane while sitting in your backyard, the chance that this might happen is quite improbable. Living in fear and fear of the unexpected are terms that may signify catastrophizing.

Example: I am never swimming in the ocean again. Someone saw a shark 20 miles offshore last week. What if it comes in and attacks me?

Your example:

6. **Personalization**—This is when you assume that everyone's actions are in reaction to you, or that you are in competition with everyone else in the world. Cues that tell you are stuck in this type of thinking are It's because of me, or Everyone else. The point is that you feel as though you must question your worth at every turn. If someone does better than you on a test, you feel 'less than.' If something bad happens, you assume that it's your fault. **Taking it personally** is a phrase that we use to describe this.

   Example: She clearly wore that dress to my birthday party because she knows I absolutely hate the color orange. She did it just to bug me.

   Your example:

7. **Control Fallacies**—This comes in two different variants, and we can fall into each type, depending on the situation. The first type is what we call the **victim type,** where you believe that you are victim of external forces, and have no power or control over your destiny. The second type is the **perpetrator type**, where you believe that you are responsible for other people's happiness—in fact that it is your job to make other people happy. Terms we use to define these types of people are people pleasers and victims. Both suffer from a distortion about how much control they actually have in their lives or on others.

   Example: It's hopeless. I'm never going to get a job in this economy. I'm not even going to try.

   Your example:

8. **Fallacy of Fairness**—This type of thinking revolves around what you have personally defined as fair, and using this definition as a measuring stick to judge others and their treatment of you. The problem is, others may not agree with your definition of fairness or even be aware that it exists! **Resentment** is frequently the result of a fallacy of fairness.

Example: Jonathan has not had me over for two weeks, and I'm not going to invite him back here until he invites me to his house first. It's not fair that it is always up to me to invite him over.

Your example:

9. **Blaming**—Ah, blaming. This is a very common distortion, where we blame others for the things that happen to us, rather than to take personal responsibility for our own choices and decisions, and acknowledge that sometimes, stuff just happens. People who blame frequently do not know how to speak up and tell others what they want or need, and in silence, let others take action only to later blame them for not responding to their (unspoken) needs. **Don't blame me!** is a frequent retort by blamers themselves.

Example: It's not my fault there's nothing on the menu I like to eat. You decided on the restaurant, not me!

Your example:

10. **Shoulds**—This is where you have an ironclad set of rules on how things should be (hamburgers should always have ketchup), how people should act (I can't believe he is wearing sandals), or think (everyone knows politicians are all idiots). Not only do you firmly believe that everyone should think and behave within these parameters without fail, you believe that you also are at fault if you fail to live up to your immutable expectations. You know you're in Shoulds when you use words like **should, ought, and must.**

Example: Everyone knows that you should eat dinner before 6 pm because it's not good to eat too close to bedtime. If you eat any later, you'll get sick.

Your example:

11. **Emotional Reasoning**—this is where you take a general feeling you are having and apply it to your entire personality. So, if you are feeling bored, then you are obviously a boring person. If you feel sick today, then you must be either dying or a hypochondriac. In other words, you allow an **emotional state**—which may be temporary—to define your entire being, for good or bad.

    Example: I am absolutely unstoppable—I have won five games of poker, and I'm on fire. I am going to take all of my savings and go to Vegas. I am certain that I will win every time!

    Your example:

12. **Fallacy of Change**—This is the expectation that if someone truly loves you, they will change for you. Two things are wrong with this thinking—one, that your feelings are more important than the other's feelings, and two, that other people control your happiness, when in fact you are the one who controls your happiness. This is a common problem in marriages, where one partner marries the other, thinking that s/he can change the other. A common phrase heard is **If you really loved me, you would...**

    Example: If you were really my friend, it wouldn't bother you that I never take a shower.

    Your example:

13. **Global Labeling**—This is the root of many racial, gender, and cultural stereotypes. Some examples include: Chinese people are bad drivers; Women take too long in the bathroom because they are so vain; Teenagers are all self-centered and rude; All police officers are corrupt; Gay men are always trying to convert straight men. Global labeling ignores contrary evidence and lumps all people of a given group in on erroneous bag. The common indicator of global labeling is the qualifier **ALL**.

Example: I was in an accident yesterday, and of course, the person who hit me was Chinese. They are such horrid drivers.

Your example:

14. **Being Right**—The only way to be is right, or at least more right than the other person, right? Insisting on being right assumes that your position is the only correct position, and that anyone who has a differing opinion is clearly wrong. While this may not sound so awful, do remember that the other person may feel equally as strongly about his or her position. Thus, no matter how strongly you feel about something, the concept of **being right is nearly always subjective**. And, if being right all the time means that you push other people out of your life, is being right all that important? If you had to choose between being happy and being right, which would you choose?

Example: I don't care what you say, all Democrats are socialist goons who want to take away all of our individual rights, and I can't possibly accept anyone who doesn't believe the same thing, even if it means I never speak to my daughter again.

Your example:

15. **Heaven's Reward Fallacy**—This is one that many people get caught up in— sometimes it's called Tit for Tat, or **playing the martyr**, meaning that there is a scoreboard somewhere, where you or someone else is keeping track of who has done what for whom. The object of this scorekeeping is either to make sure that the 'score' is 'even' (I do for you, and then you do for me), or that if we do lots of things for someone that they will 'owe' us their love and constancy out of a sense of guilt.

Example: My son is so ungrateful. I worked my fingers to the bone for him all of my life, and now he won't even cancel a silly vacation to come visit when his aunt is in town. After everything I've done for him!

Your example:

Now, go back and review the 15 types of distorted thinking, and write down the ones that you use most frequently, and jot down some ideas of how you can 'rethink' them:

1.

2.

3.

4.

5.

Getting Stuck in Negativity

I have met very few people in life who never got stuck in a negative frame of mind. I can think of just two people who could always look on the positive side of life. Most of us get stuck in that Eeyore, gray-cloud thinking from time to time, and so it's useful for all of us to be mindful of this state, to be able to identify when we're stuck, and to learn how to get unstuck.

Most of us get stuck in situations where we have had difficulty being successful in the past. Sometimes, we might be in a completely new situation, and still get stuck—because of past failures we perceive to be similar. The first step is to identify that you are stuck—which can be surprisingly difficult to do. All of us are very good at 'fooling' ourselves into believing that our thoughts are completely rational.

How do you know if you're stuck? Ask yourself if your responses are:

1. Based on always, never, should? (polarized thinking, overgeneralization)

2. Based on emotional responses such as I can't or won't be allowed? (personalization)

3. Based on everyone else's interference? (blaming, control fallacy)

4. Based on my needing to being right?

Spending some time really looking and evaluating your responses critically and analytically will help you identify if you are stuck. But remember, the more resistant we are to looking at something in a new way, the more stuck we are—we have an emotional investment in *not* looking at the situation and *not* changing, because change is often scary.

Fear of Change

Most of us fear change—physically and emotionally, we are built for stasis, or 'standing still.' All of us like to have some things in our lives remain the same, because it is how we build structure and some level of comfortable normalcy in our lives. However—as the saying goes, the only constant is change, and so we need to learn to be less fearful of trying new things and doing things in a different way. This is particularly important when what we have been doing does not work, or when our behavior is impacting us in a negative way.

This begs the question—if we know that our behavior is causing trouble in our lives, why would we *not* want to change that behavior? The answer is often simple— because change would require that we take full responsibility and accountability for our lives, which in turn would mean that if something went wrong—*we are responsible.* No more blaming, no more externalizing, the virtual buck stops with us.

That acceptance of personal responsibility is very uncomfortable for many of us. We don't want to be completely responsible because it's a huge weight to bear. But the bottom line is, we are *already* completely responsible anyway—we just need to acknowledge it and accept it.

So, take a few minutes now, and try to identify a few of your 'favorite' things you are resistant to change—things you know you need to change, but don't:

1.

2.

3.

4.

5.

Now, write down *why* you think you are resistant to change these same things:

1.

2.

3.

4.

5.

When you review the list above, you might see that some of the things you don't want to change are not really important to you right now. Or are they? Be careful to not 'fool yourself' into believing that something that really is important to you, isn't!

Silencing Negative Thoughts

When you are able to ascertain that you are in fact experiencing negative or distorted thinking, the next question is: how do you stop? This may be a hard question to answer, because as noted above, many of us are quite wedded to our negative thoughts because then we do not have to take responsibility. And if we take responsibility and things don't go well, we have to blame ourselves. Right?

Well, actually, wrong! The need to blame is often the crux of the problem. Why do we feel we need to blame someone if things don't go well—yes, we need to take responsibility, and we need to try, but we don't have to blame anyone, even ourselves, if things do not work out. We simply need to learn from our experiences, figure out a different path, and try again. Where does blame fit into this equation? It doesn't!

Yes, this sounds simple, but we are so used to assigning blame that it is very difficult to do this in practice, especially if blame has been a part of our family system over the years. Silencing negative thoughts, then, takes work and practice. Here are some ways that people have been successful at silencing negative thoughts:

- ❏ Talk therapy
- ❏ Cognitive-Behavior therapy
- ❏ Hypnotherapy
- ❏ Group therapy
- ❏ Meditation
- ❏ Relaxation tapes
- ❏ Self-reflection
- ❏ Affirmations

All of these are good ways to reduce the 'back seat driver' in our brains that guide our negative thinking. Would any of them work for you? Have you tried any of them, and did they work? Which ones would you be willing to try, or try again? Put a check mark by the ideas above that sound appealing or useful.

How to Believe

I will tell you a secret. The bottom line in all of these techniques is that you have to *believe* that you *can* change and that you are *worth* the effort to change. Let me say that again—you have to believe that you can change and that you are worth it.

Believing that change is possible, and believing that you are worth the effort, may be the hardest part of moving from distorted thinking into more rational thoughts. For people who have a difficult time with this, group therapy and ongoing affirmations seem to work best. You need to be continually reminded—until you believe yourself— that you are in fact worth the effort, and that you can change if you wish.

Are You Worth the Effort?

One of the biggest problems most of us face when we are struggling is the sense that we really don't need to try harder, or try to find better solutions, because we have 'always' failed in the past, and so we will certainly fail again this time. Here's a little exercise you can do to better understand how distorted thinking works. See if you can fill in some of the blanks below.

Situation	Distorted Thinking	Reality
John has no plans for Friday	No one ever calls me up, and when I call them to go out, they are always busy. I hate my life.	No one called me up this weekend, but then, I didn't call anyone either. I did go out last weekend with a couple of friends and we had a good time.
Sam got a D on a paper	I worked my ass off on this paper, and I got a lousy D. There is no reason for me to try any more.	I started the paper two days before it was due, though I had known about it for weeks.
Susan overslept	I can't ever get up in the morning—why bother trying?	
Raveesh has not found a job	I sent out four resumes, but did not follow up on them.	
Luis has to babysit his brother		
Anne wants a new dress		

You get the picture. We often use distorted thinking when we don't like the reality that we could have done something different, and use it as a way of giving up, making excuses for a poor outcome, or of making something appear to be worse than it really is.

Another way we short-circuit ourselves is by blaming others. We frequently do this when we don't want to look at how we are responsible for creating a happy life. It is always easy to blame the situation, someone else, etc., rather than acknowledge that there is something we could be doing differently. Let's have a look.

Situation	Blaming	Reality
John has no plans for Friday	My friends are all a bunch of losers and don't care about me. It's their fault I have no life.	No one called me up this weekend, but then, I didn't call anyone either. I did go out last weekend with a couple of friends and we had a good time.
Sam got a D on a paper	The teacher never gives us enough time to do these papers, and then expects miracles.	I started the paper two days before it was due, though I had known about it for weeks.
Susan overslept	I keep telling you I need a new alarm clock! This one doesn't work!	
Raveesh has not found a job	I sent out four resumes, but did not follow up on them.	
Luis has to babysit his brother		
Anne wants a new dress		

Our Own Worst Enemy—Us!

Sad but true, we are often our own worst enemies when it comes to getting stuck, thinking in distorted, useless ways, and sitting on the pity pot, apparently enjoying our misery. We let ourselves get bogged down in unimportant details, we let ourselves get dragged into dramas we don't need to be part of, we find ways to waste our time rather than making the most out of the one life we have been given. We all do it. Yep, me too.

Which makes me ask—*What is up with that?*

Life hands us plenty of obstacles to deal with—why on earth would we put *more* obstacles in our way? We each have our own reasons, but usually it's because we don't believe in ourselves enough, we are not kind enough to put ourselves first, and make our own dreams come true. Very little is impossible if we are willing to put ourselves out there, and really try with everything we've got. But trying takes effort, it takes courage, and it takes constancy. Which means that the harder something is to attain, we have to want it all that much more to do the hard work necessary to achieve it.

When my son was about four years old, we were vacationing at a lake up in the mountains. We had just finished lunch at a picnic table, and he wanted a Popsicle®. The snack shack was about 20 feet away from our table, and so I put a dollar bill on the table and told him to go buy one. He was terrified and told me that I had to come with him. He was by nature shy, had social communication challenges, and had never bought anything by himself before. I told him that I knew he could do this, and then explained to him, step by step, how to buy the Popsicle®, what to say, and what to do. He persisted in wanting me to come with him, and was visibly upset, but I refused to go with him. This went on for several minutes, when I finally asked him one simple question: *How badly do you want a Popsicle®?*

He finally screwed up his courage, and bought the Popsicle® by himself. I am sure that it tasted infinitely better than if I had bought it for him.

Your Thought Management Profile

As you've learned in this chapter, it's one thing to know what to do in terms of organizing yourself, your space, your time, and how to make decisions, sequence tasks, and so forth. But it is entirely a different subject when it comes down to—*will you do it?* We all get caught up in negative thought patterns, no one is immune. But, the difference between those who can succeed at the tasks they set out for themselves, and those who do not, may well reside in the ability to manage one's own thoughts.

Go through these exercises and see if you can identify what your particular challenges are, in the past, present, and potentially in the future, and then identify how you can overcome them.

My Thought Management Skills		Example of Use
Thought Screening	❑ Good ❑ Fair ❑ So-So	
Thought Cessation	❑ Good ❑ Fair ❑ So-So	
Thought Sorting	❑ Good ❑ Fair ❑ So-So	
Thought Running	❑ Good ❑ Fair ❑ So-So	
My Distorted Thinking Challenges		**What I Can Do To Stop This Thinking**
Filtering	❑ I do this ❑ Sometimes ❑ Not really	
Polarized Thinking	❑ I do this ❑ Sometimes ❑ Not really	
Overgeneralization	❑ I do this ❑ Sometimes ❑ Not really	

My Distorted Thinking Challenges		What I Can Do To Stop This Thinking
Mind Reading	❑ I do this ❑ Sometimes ❑ Not really	
Catastrophizing	❑ I do this ❑ Sometimes ❑ Not really	
Personalization	❑ I do this ❑ Sometimes ❑ Not really	
Control Fallacies	❑ I do this ❑ Sometimes ❑ Not really	
Fallacy of Fairness	❑ I do this ❑ Sometimes ❑ Not really	
Blaming	❑ I do this ❑ Sometimes ❑ Not really	
Shoulds	❑ I do this ❑ Sometimes ❑ Not really	
Emotional Reasoning	❑ I do this ❑ Sometimes ❑ Not really	
Fallacy of Change	❑ I do this ❑ Sometimes ❑ Not really	
Global Labeling	❑ I do this ❑ Sometimes ❑ Not really	
Being Right	❑ I do this ❑ Sometimes ❑ Not really	
Heaven's Reward	❑ I do this ❑ Sometimes ❑ Not really	

Obstacle Management

Stuff happens. It just does. Call it Murphy's Law, bad luck or timing, or whatever, but sometimes we find ourselves in a major pile of doggie doo. Obstacles, however, are not necessarily the end point.

What To Do?

We know that sometimes the worst happens, and things go really, really wrong. Even with really careful planning, you cannot always succeed—the economy turns for the worse when you're in your second month of a new business; your dream of becoming a stem cell researcher is dashed because of new, restrictive laws suddenly passing legislation severely curtailing new projects; you cannot go to your first-choice college because your father lost his job, and can no longer afford it. What do you do?

After you've gotten over the shock and sadness of having your original goals thwarted, you essentially have three possible courses of action, listed from least desirable to most desirable:

1. Give up totally

2. Start over on a new goal

3. Reframe your goal

Here's a real-life scenario that I want you to think about as you read through this information. I had planned on being a high school teacher in California and was almost done with my degree at UC Berkeley. I had already applied for graduate school to get my teacher's credential. I wanted to teach high school English—it was my passion. Then, two quarters before I graduated, Proposition 13 passed in California, and hundreds of teachers were laid off. There were no jobs, and would not be any jobs in California for many years to come. Everything I had planned for was then out the window and I had to come up with a different plan.

Giving Up—Least Desirable Solution

In the face of a major monkey wrench in our plans, many of us will be so devastated by the change of events that it will cause us to simply stop and give up. Having lost 'the wind in our sails,' we give up, feeling dejected, and lost. This is very normal behavior—even if it doesn't help us very often.

There are times when giving up gracefully may be the right answer, but before doing so, you need to make sure that you are not giving up just because of your emotional state, and that you have really explored the options that may be available to you. In short, you need to stop and think carefully before taking action. We'll talk about how to do that in a bit.

Remember that we cannot achieve everything we set out to do and that some failure is inevitable. Don't lose hope, and don't lose the lessons learned.

*Describe a time in your life when you gave up:*_____

_____

_____

Starting Over—More Desirable Solution

Frequently, one of the better options is to simply pick up and move on—and start over. Sometimes that's the best option because you can't reframe, and you don't want to give up. Other times, it may be that you just need to cut your ties and try something completely different. Starting over could be the best way to breathe fresh air into your life—or, it could also be a pattern of not hanging in there long enough to work through the normal issues of any goal's progress.

So for example, if you were trying to go into stem cell research but no longer could because research had been halted, you could go back to school and get a certificate from a community college in a related medical or research field that was flourishing. You didn't give up, you started a new path.

Describe a time in your life when you started over on a goal: _____

_____

_____

Reframing—Most Desirable Solution

This is often the best solution—reframing is taking your current goal and tweaking it—a little or a lot—without giving up on the whole idea entirely. So, if you were studying bio-chem, and new laws made stem cell research undoable, you could look into the other areas that biochem can be applied in the business and research world, and wait out the political storm. Or, you could consider moving to Europe where stem cell research is still legal and moving forward. In short, reframing is taking the current situation, and finding a way around the obstacle in question.

Describe a time when you 'reframed' a situation to keep moving forward: _____

_____

_____

Now, go back and think about my experience with wanting to become a teacher. What options do you think I had? I could have gone forward with my teaching degree and moved out of California to find a job (**reframing**), or could have started over and find another way to use my English Literature degree other than teaching (**starting over**), or I could have given up on the idea of teaching or using my degree. Ultimately, I **gave up**—I chose another field entirely (cooking), and then became a technical writer years later, which used my English degree. Later still, I returned to school to get my Masters and now work with the teenagers I had wanted to teach thirty years ago. Over time, even giving up sometimes turns out to be reframing or starting over—I now do very much the work I had wanted to do fresh out of college, it just took me longer to work my way to it.

Planning For Potential Obstacles

One way to avoid obstacles is to plan for them! I realize that that sounds really bizarre—to plan for an obstacle—but the truth is that many obstacles can be planned for if you do a little critical thinking. We've learned quite a few techniques already in previous chapters to analyze a situation—urgent vs. important, natural sequences, dependencies. We talked about needed structures and support that you might need. Now, we're going to apply the things we've learned to analyze ways to prepare for the unexpected.

❏ **Scenario One**—Jonathan is planning on taking a trip next summer (after the Winter and Spring quarters) to Los Angeles to do a four-week internship at a Hollywood studio doing digital animation. It's a dream of a lifetime for him, as he has always wanted to get into animation. He needs to earn and save about $1500 to pay for his travel expenses, lodging, and food while he's there, he has to complete two more classes in digital animation before he will qualify for the internship, and he has to get at least a B in the classes. He has been provisionally accepted into the program, based on passing grades in these two classes, and earning enough money.

What should Jonathan do to ensure that nothing goes wrong with this plan? What obstacles should he plan for, and how should he circumvent them? Think sequencing and dependencies! Write down your thoughts here:

❑ **Scenario Two**—Samantha is at her first job as a photographer and has been given a really great assignment to work a wedding. It is up in San Francisco at 7 pm on a Friday evening, and the wedding will be held outside at the Legion of Honor. She's never been there, but will get the directions off of Google Maps. Her boss said he will send her a complete list of things to pack—which cameras, filters, lenses, types of film, etc.—a few days before the wedding date, and reminded her that she needs to be professionally dressed for the event.

What does Samantha need to plan for, and where are the potential pitfalls here? What can she do to overcome them? Remember dependencies and think method of loci (walkthrough)?

❑ **Scenario Three**—Lucia wants to get a new apartment, and thinks she has found the perfect one. It's a three-bedroom, and costs about $400 more a month than her current one-bedroom apartment, so she has found two people to rent the other rooms. One is a good friend (Johnna) who has wanted to move out of her family's home, and the other is a student she has met at the local community college—Sandra something. Because Lucia is the only one who has ever rented an apartment before, she plans on signing the lease on her own, so that they will just check her credit, which is very good. She has collected part of the deposit from Johnna and has her portion, too, but hasn't gotten the deposit yet from Sandra. Lucia is going to give notice tomorrow on her current apartment in order to avoid paying for additional month, and then will call the new landlord and go over to sign the new lease. She really, really doesn't want to lose this apartment; it is so perfect.

THE CEO OF SELF

Pitfalls? Issues? How would you handle it differently? Think sequencing and dependencies.

_____

_____

_____

_____

_____

_____

- ❑ **Scenario Four**—Flavio is taking a heavy load this quarter, trying to finish up his studies so he can graduate a bit early. He's having a bit of a challenge keeping up on his studies and projects/papers, but has come up with a strategy of focusing on one of his three classes every day, and putting off the homework for the other classes, working them each in sequence. For the most part, this works, but he has two large research projects coming up in two weeks that he has not yet started. Meanwhile, Flavio's cousin has offered to give him his old car because he just bought a new one—but he has to go to Seattle to pick it up, and drive it home by next weekend at the latest. Flavio figures he can get all of his work on the projects done, and go up the weekend after next, right before the papers are due. He immediately purchased a non-refundable, one-way ticket so that he could be sure to go.

Where is this plan likely to fall apart? What can Flavio do to make sure it does not fall apart? Think prioritization and urgent versus important.

_____

_____

_____

_____

_____

_____

Three Golden Rules to Manage a Crisis

In each of the above scenarios, something very well may go wrong, just like in everyday life. The exercises are meant to show you where things go wrong, and to start thinking about how to fix each situation.

When things go wrong, there are three golden rules to remember:

1. **Ensure a crisis does not happen.** Many crises are avoidable with proper planning and foresight. What it takes is time—time to think through your plan start to finish, and identify any areas that might be problematic. Think through how you might resolve those issues in advance, or develop contingency plans. Taking this time to 'pre-think' the situation may save you a lot of time and heartache later. Note that this is NOT the same as obsessive worrying—this is thinking through your plan, two or three times.

Write an example from the scenarios on the previous pages:

2. **Stop. Think. THEN act.** Bad, reactive decisions will always make the situation worse. Period, full stop. Better to take the time to think through the situation and carefully weigh options before taking remedial action. It may seem like it is urgent to react, but ask yourself if it is important to act right away.

Write an example from the scenarios on the previous pages:

3. **Prioritize your actions.** Much time is wasted in the heat of the moment by trying to resolve a situation that is unresolvable, or by doing things that end up making the situation worse. Use critical thinking to ascertain what is really important at this point in time, and work on those things first.

Write an example from the scenarios on the previous pages:

Preparing For the Unforeseeable

Okay, so life does throw us some curve balls from time to time—we are not the only ones who can screw up our plans! But, even if you cannot plan for all obstacles that fall in your path, you can plan mentally and emotionally for dealing with setbacks, pitfalls, and detours.

How do you do that? By building resiliency in yourself—building the sense that no matter what pops up, you can handle it—you WILL handle it. This doesn't mean that you won't have the occasional emotional upheaval, that you won't ever be disappointed, that you won't sometimes feel like giving up. What it does mean is that in short-order you pull yourself back together and move on.

Being resilient is frequently a conscious choice of endurance—of having more lasting power than your opponent, more creativity to overcome the obstacle, more guts to drive forward and keep going. All of this is internal—all of it comes from within. And it all starts with positive thinking.

So, we're going to do a little exercise. Below are the beginnings of a saying—your job is to finish these in a way that shows resiliency and determination.

The only failure is_____

Success is a matter of_____

Determination comes from_____

My goals are worth_____

The highest achievement is_____

No one ever_____

Some people believe_____

I have never_____

The value of my life will be judged by_____

Now, **circle** your favorite saying!

Are You Stuck?

Even if your life is going along flawlessly, there are probably one or two aspects you would change—maybe working harder in school, saving more money, spending more time with friends. These are pretty easy things to fix. You simply do some tweaking, change a few things in your life, and there you go.

Or do you? One thing that is not always easy to do is to identify where and why you are stuck—why you stopped doing so well in school, where your money is going, and why you aren't spending as much time with friends as you'd like.

Sometimes we are stuck because the environment doesn't respond the way we had anticipated it—we thought a particular class would be easy, and it isn't. We thought we could easily save a hundred dollars a month, but our rent went up. And so on.

As we've talked about in the past, some of these things we can plan for, and some we cannot. There are, of course, many things that hinder us in our goals that we can control—and in fact are responsible for. These are the tricky 'stuck' places to uncover and deal with. Are we really working up to our potential in our classwork? Are we spending money on silly stuff we don't really want or need? Are your friends really busy, or do we just not take the time to call them and set up times to get together?

So, take a few minutes, and think about where you might be stuck, and why. Some of the reasons may include:

- ❏ Lack of motivation (the goal wasn't really that important to you)
- ❏ Not believing that change is really important (not bought in)
- ❏ Fear of risk (trying new things)
- ❏ Fear of failure (risking but not succeeding)
- ❏ Fear of succeeding (which would require change and letting go of old habits)
- ❏ Anger or annoyance at having to change
- ❏ Concern about what your change might mean to someone else

If you are stuck in any aspect, write about it here, and try to describe why you are stuck:

_____

_____

_____

_____

_____

_____

Perseverance—What Is It?

In order to move through the obstacles in life, we need perseverance. But what does that mean? From *The American Heritage Dictionary*:

per·se·ver·ance

n.

1. Steady persistence in adhering to a course of action, a belief, or a purpose; steadfastness.

And to give you an idea of why perseverance is important, let's look to a few people who might know something about it.

> To be nobody but yourself — in a world which is doing its best, night and day, to make you everybody else — means to fight the hardest battle any human being can fight, and never stop fighting.
>
> — ee cummings (American poet and playwright)

> This thing that we call "failure" is not falling down, but the staying down.
>
> — Mary Pickford

> Many of life's failures are people who do not realize how close they were to success when they gave up.
>
> —Thomas Edison

We may know what perseverance means, and most of us have experienced perseverance in ourselves at one time or another, but we may not take much time to think about it and its ramifications on our lives. What does it mean to keep trying against all odds, and what does it mean to accept defeat at some point? Is there a way we can identify when we should keep going, and when we should give up? And how do we continue to be motivated to continue in the face of adversity and failure?

These are all very important questions, and none of them have hard and fast answers—most of them are very much in the realm of 'it depends.' Not exactly a nice cut and dried answer is it?

Consider this: Thomas Edison tried over 10,000 combinations before he finally hit on a working lightbulb. How would life be different if he had given up? So, how did he find the perseverance to try so many times? Most likely he *knew* that he was close— he knew intellectually, in his gut, and by intuition that what he was trying to do was reasonable, and that the answer lay in his getting the exact materials balanced so that they would work in harmony.

What else did Edison have going for him?

1. He knew exactly what his goal was—to create an object that would illuminate when electricity passed through it.

2. He knew what materials would likely work.

3. He had a workshop where he could do all of his work.

4. He had assistants helping him.

5. He knew that perfecting a practical lightbulb was not the only goal—he also had to invent/perfect:

   ❑ the parallel circuit
   ❑ an improved dynamo
   ❑ the underground conductor network
   ❑ the devices for maintaining constant voltage
   ❑ safety fuses and insulating materials
   ❑ light sockets with on-off switches

So, his was not a simple, single invention—in fact, he had to create an entirely new *business framework*—generating electricity—in order for the relatively simple invention of the lightbulb to actually work. Talk about the need for perseverance!

Using everything you have learned in this book so far, write down five things that Edison must have used or been conscious of in order to make the lightbulb a success. This is an open book exercise, so go back through this book, and see what all fits.

1.

2.

3.

4.

5.

Now, take a few more minutes to consider how this project could have failed—what might have gone wrong, or caused him to rightfully pull the plug on the project and give up:

1.

2.

3.

4.

5.

When we think about researchers, inventors, entrepreneurs, we are talking about some of the most persevering individuals on earth. How many years will it take to find a cure for AIDs or for cancer? How did the heart pacemaker get developed? How did Donald Trump build a mega-empire? Very few people get where they want to be without many, many setbacks, lots of hard work, and of course—perseverance.

What Perseverance Is Not

There's a joke in the mental health community that goes something like this: Doing the same thing over and over and over again and expecting different results is the sign of mental illness. And, to a large degree, this is true of human behavior. We continue to stay up too late, and somehow magically expect to awake the next day refreshed. We argue with our parents, and we expect the relationship to go smoothly. We forget to let the dog out before we leave for work or school, and expect him not to pee all over the house.

Truly, none of these are examples of perseverance, but examples of wishful thinking, that somehow things will magically change if we simply will them to do so.

Now, if we have to stay up late, and we really need to be refreshed the next day, perseverance would say—find a way to take a nap during the day, or accept that on this one day you will be tired. But don't expect to do it over the long haul. Or, I need to have this difficult conversation with my parents—they won't like it, and it will be hard to remain calm—but I have to do it in order to get what I need. Or, I have to leave the dog in the house this week because they are fixing the fence, so I better have someone come over during the day to let him out—otherwise he'll pee all over, no fault of his own.

Those *are* examples of perseverance—which often requires advanced planning and anticipating obstacles, as we have talked about in earlier lessons. This is completely different than just going about your life in the same way every day and expecting things to be different—it just won't happen unless we plan for that difference, understand when things have gone awry, and make adjustments so that next time we have a better shot at success.

Perseverance Chart

Pretty much everyone has had to persevere to accomplish something in their lives. Take a few minutes and work through this sheet—in the middle, write down a time when you had to persevere to accomplish something. Work your

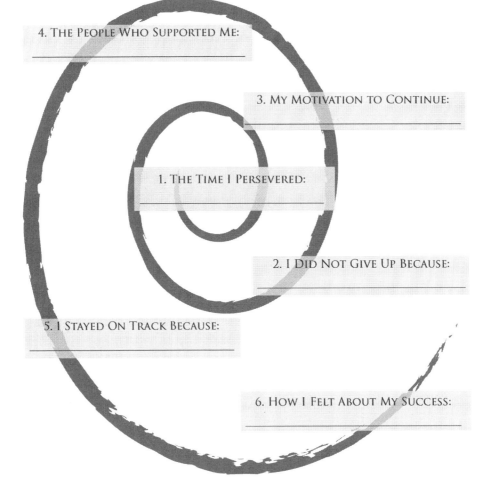

4. The People Who Supported Me:

3. My Motivation to Continue:

1. The Time I Persevered:

2. I Did Not Give Up Because:

5. I Stayed On Track Because:

6. How I Felt About My Success:

way around the outside boxes and answer the questions. Take your time and really think deeply about your answers.

When you look at this chart, a few things may become clear. First, persevering is rarely done in a vacuum—we generally have people supporting us. Additionally, we may have had to deal with some 'naysayers'—folks who were certain we could not accomplish our goals. We had to find internal (or external) motivators to keep us going, and we may have had to use self-affirmations, reframing, and other tools as well. As we went along working on our goals, we may have had to do some reframing when we hit an obstacle or unexpected event.

In short, having perseverance really means using all of the tools that we have learned to date to keep on track—it is the quality that keeps us from giving up 'when the going gets rough.'

What Can't You Do?

One of the best ways to determine what you can do is to determine what you cannot do. The trick is to define the things that you really cannot do—not the things you won't do, don't want to do, or don't care about—because those things are immediately meaningless.

So, think about it for a few minutes—is there anything you really, really want to do that you don't think you can do? Write them down here:

1.

2.

3.

4.

5.

In the past, things I really wanted included being a singer, and becoming a director at the company where I work. I had to come to a place of acceptance that I would do neither. Instead, my son is now a singer, and I'm the CEO of my own company. Life has a funny way of working sometimes!

Perseveration—How Is It Different?

Once again, from From *The American Heritage Dictionary*:

per·sev·er·a·tion

n.

1. Psychology

    a. Uncontrollable repetition of a particular response, such as a word, phrase, or gesture, despite the absence or cessation of a stimulus, usually caused by brain injury or other organic disorder.

    b. The tendency to continue or repeat an act or activity after the cessation of the original stimulus.

In psychology, and particularly with folks on the autistic spectrum, perseveration typically means being completely enthralled with one thing to the exclusion of all else (or, nearly all else). In practicality, people on the spectrum may actually be engrossed in more than one thing, and frequently will change focus from one object or activity to another over time. For folks on the spectrum, perseveration of this type is also probably soothing and comfortable—to absolutely master one thing in its entirety.

Perseveration can also come in milder forms—sticking with something like a virtual pit bull when that something is no longer practical or reasonable due to shifting circumstances. That's the type of perseveration we're talking about today.

Sometimes it's a fine line between persevering and perseverating. How do we know that it's time to give up, regroup, and move on? How can we be sure that if we didn't try just one more month or week or day, even, that we couldn't be successful this time? The truth is, it is often very difficult to know exactly when the perfect time to call it quits is—and some of us will quit too soon (before failure becomes apparent to others), and others will quit too late (long past the time failure was obvious to those around us).

Following Old Rules

One theory explains perseveration as an inflexibility of the mind when presented with a change of circumstances, something novel, or something presented in a new way—in other words, our brains want to follow the existing—or old—rules, rather than switch to the new ones. Even if the person knows cognitively that they *should* move on to the new rules, they simply can't move the new task into their working memory—the old one stays stuck. The brain literally seems to be unable to let new information into our working memory (the part of our brain used to execute tasks) instead of reconnecting to other parts of the brain that identify and retrieve new information. My favorite way of describing this problem is the wind-up toy—you wind it up, and off it goes, moving steadily in one direction. Until it hits a wall. Then, it just keeps going, trying to move through the wall. It can't turn itself around and move in a new direction—it just keeps going and going and going, hoping the wall will disappear and it can move forward. Which ain't gonna happen!

So, how do we build flexibility? How do we learn to let go and move on? Hmmm, pretty tough question. There are two halves to this answer—one is emotional and the other is functional. The emotional part of perseveration is learning to let go of the known, and to try the unknown, which may cause fear and unease. The functional part of perseveration is teaching our brains to think in new ways—to literally let new information in.

Letting Go

Learning to let go of what is known and look at things in a new way is an emotional task. Wse may need to look at things that are no longer working in our lives and make changes. This can cause us to be fearful as we leave the realm of the known and travel into the unknown. Our rational minds know that change is needed, but our emotional minds are fearful that giving up our current state may cause us pain. So, we tend to stick to the known, which, while dysfunctional, is at least familiar.

In 1937, the noted theologian Reinhold Niebuhr wrote what is now known as the Serenity Prayer :

> *May I have the serenity to accept the things I cannot change,*
> *The courage to change the things I can,*
> *And the wisdom to know the difference.*[1]

Although this 'prayer' is now associated with self-help and groups like Alcoholics Anonymous, it really does sum up the act of appropriate letting go—knowing what you can and cannot change, and making the changes that you can actually put into place. Many of us spend years—even lifetimes—trying to change things that we ultimately cannot change. We try to be people we are not. We try to change those whom we love to be different people (parents are very good at this!). We try to make

---

1   Retrieved from the New York Times, January 23, 2010 http://www.nytimes.com/2009/11/28/us/28prayer.html.

bureaucracies care about us as individuals. As many health and wellness experts note, we try to 'beat the system.'

> If our wish is something that is not within our control, then it is perhaps best to accept what is, and let go of that desire. In the simplest of situations, it is a merely a matter of adjusting one's thinking. For example, if you are in a hurry and find yourself stuck in a traffic jam, the reality is there is nothing you can do to make traffic move more quickly no matter how hard you may wish otherwise. Tying oneself in emotional knots is not helpful nor healthful. Let go of the worry of being late. Instead, have the presence of mind to accept your current reality, and be at peace. The difference between being at peace and being extremely stressed comes down to the difference in how you think. Nothing has changed in terms of the physical reality of the situation, but the hormone and neurotransmitter response in your body will be radically different.[2]

Others of us spend our lives passing over opportunity after opportunity all because we do not want to change the status quo, upset the apple cart. We hang on so tightly to what is known, that we cannot stretch and try new things for fear of potential loss.

The problem is that when you are attached to the results, your sense of well-being becomes compromised. When this happens, you are actually less effective and less able to create the outcomes you desire. Your possibilities are eclipsed by clinging and grasping after a result.

One of the things that makes it very difficult to let go is the feeling of pain. You might feel pain about the state of the environment, or pain about the loss of a loved one. You might have a broken heart because of the chaos in the world, the loss of your financial nest egg, the loss of a dream, or the loss of a loved one.

Whatever the case, in order to create the life you want, in order to make the impact you want, in order to become the person you want to be, you must heal the broken parts of your heart.

> As you heal your heart from the disappointment, the grief, the loneliness, the pain, the frustration - whatever - you will discover that you can pursue your dreams with passion, but you have no need to cling and grasp after a particular outcome. You can set an intention, let it go, and live the life you know you are meant to live.[3]

---

2   Vreni Gurd, blog retrieved January 23, 2012, http://live.ezezine.com/displaypost.ez?f=./posts/2012/01/221-2012.01.08.07.00-html-.jpd.

3   Intent.com, retrieved July 22, 2011 intent.com.

Letting go of what we know in order to find a new or better path is hard. But it is the key to becoming 'unstuck'—we have to train ourselves to try new—and harder—tasks in order to live our lives fully. The key is to set an intention, and follow that, learning to adapt and change your specific goals along the way as opportunities arise, as your life changes, and as the old no longer works.

Fight, Flight, or *Cope!*

From traffic to job stress to bills and school, most of us face many stressors throughout the day. Our bodies react to this stress with the fight or flight response, which alters different functions in our bodies temporarily so we have a jolt of energy we can use to fight or run from a perceived threat. While this in itself isn't a problem for our health, many of us repeatedly experience this response throughout the day with an absence of accompanying calmness, resulting in chronic stress and a constant hyper-arousal of our body's stress response. (Simply put: our bodies always think they're in danger, and this can cause a great deal of wear and tear.) Over time, we end up more susceptible to illness, both mental and physical, as a result, and the experience of all this stress (let alone the health problems that can result from it) can hinder our happiness.

Fortunately, there are some simple ways to calm your body quickly and counteract your body's stress response so that your body has a chance to recover from daily stresses and you feel more at peace. The following short-term stress relievers can be quite helpful:

❑ **Breathing Exercises:** Take a few deep breaths. Breathing in 'relaxation' and breathing out the stress you feel, and expanding your diaphragm (rather than lifting your shoulders) as you breathe can help you to feel calm very quickly. This is a great one to try, as it can be done anywhere at any time, and requires no special equipment.

❑ **Reframing:** Reframe your experience. A lot of the stress we feel has to do with our perception of what's going on—remember, the fight or flight response is triggered by perceived threat, not actual threat. If you can get into the practice of viewing more experiences as challenges rather than threats, you can remain calm and interested in finding a solution, rather than stressed and scattered.

❑ **Take a Break:** If you give yourself a few minutes to calm down and clear your head, you can often calm down your physiology. Taking a short walk changes your scenery, gets your blood circulating, and helps blow off steam, so this can be a beneficial way to take a break. However, just allowing a little space between you and what stresses you, can often allow you to calm down and feel more prepared to deal.

In addition to these 'quick fix' strategies, it's also vital to have some regular stress relieving practices, so that you feel less stressed overall, and the little things don't impact you as much. The following are some of the best stress relief habits for overall stress management.

- ❑ **Meditation:** You have probably already heard of meditation as a useful stress management technique, and for good reason: meditation offers benefits for people while it's being practiced, but some evidence shows that it can also provide protective benefits so that future stresses don't bother you as much. Coupled with the fact that meditation can be done by virtually anyone, anywhere, the practice of meditation is a very useful stress management technique!

- ❑ **Yoga:** Yoga has many health-promoting benefits, so it's great for your body and your mind. Yoga can combine the benefits of meditation, breathing exercises and exercise, and provides a way to get into a different frame of mind and just feel good in the end.

- ❑ **Music:** For very busy people, even a more passive stress relief activity like listening to music can provide some useful stress management benefits overall. Music affects your body as well as your frame of mind, and can help you feel less stressed as you go about your other activities. Playing it in the morning as you get ready, in the car as you commute, or when you get home and unwind from a stressful day can all contribute to overall stress relief.

There are other things you can do as well, of course, depending on what your lifestyle is, and what your interests are—but these are good starts.

List five things you might be willing to try in the next week, when things get hairy or stressful:

1.

2.

3.

4.

5.

Dealing With It

As I'm finishing up this book, many years after I started it, I can reflect back on many trials and tribulations that have come—and gone. For quite some time, my biggest obstacle was money, and I spent many sleepless nights wondering how I was going to make payroll, pay the rent for my office, cover other business expenses—and have enough left over to pay myself enough to cover my family's living expenses.

I learned (or, relearned) a couple of very important life lessons. The first one I wrote down and taped to my monitor, so that I would see it each and every workday. It simply said:

Failure is not an option.

And it wasn't. I was not going to go back to my previous career which I now hated, I was not going to shut down my company and go look for a job working for someone else (which would be hard to do, as the work I do is very specialized, with only a handful of people in the country doing it). And I was not going to just give up. I *had* to keep going forward. I *had* to succeed.

The second life lesson I had to relearn is that no matter how much energy I put into worrying about how my company was doing, it was not going to change the outcome. I was either going to succeed or not, based on the hard work I put into the company, not based on the worry I wasted on my bottom line. This did not mean that I could be a spendthrift and waste money, and it did not mean that I didn't have to exert monumental effort to increase my income and reduce my expenses, but I had to properly focus my energy away from worry, and into the job. I had, in short, to deal with it.

When you are looking over your shoulder, worrying about what is going to happen next, ask yourself—*what can I be doing in this moment to ensure that the thing I worry most about does not happen?* And then do it!

Your Obstacle Management Profile

Nearing the end of this book, take some time to go through how you deal with obstacles in your life:

How I can handle obstacles	
Plan for them	
Reframe	
Start over	
Give up	
Ways I can get stuck	
Lack of motivation	
Don't believe I can do it	
Fear of risk/failure/success	
Anger at change	
Concern for another person	
How do I move forward	
When have I persevered?	
When have I perseverated?	
How could I tell the difference?	

On Becoming the CEO of Self

Life goes by quickly and there is rarely enough time to do all the things we want, need, and should do. Because of that simple fact, we need to make the best use of the time we have—not searching for keys we have misplaced, not redoing homework because we can't find the original we already did, not spending time staring at our computer unable to figure out how to write a business proposal.

What we *should* be doing is getting our essential work done as quickly and effectively as possible, so that we can go about doing the things that give us true joy—whether that's the 'fun' part of school, windsurfing, painting, volunteering, playing *Gears of War*—it really doesn't matter. We need and deserve joy in our lives beyond hard work.

Unfortunately, with more demands on our time, we have less and less time for joy, and many of us (myself included) become slaves to our work, our chores, and our errands, to the extent that we can't seem to ever get to the fun stuff. We speed through the week at 100 miles per hour, crash into the weekend, run around like crazy people, and then fall into bed on Sunday night—only to do it all again.

For my generation, part of becoming the *CEO of Self* means letting go of some of the things I used to have time to do—a perfectly clean and picked-up home and a beautiful garden year-round. Christmas cards, fabulous parties several times a year. Volunteering for every event at my children's schools.

But along the way, I made the decision to start my own company, and work the requisite long hours instead, and it's true: I really cannot have it all at this point of my life. My children, my sweetheart, my family, my pets are where I focus my free time, and in rare moments, reading, movies, cooking, and gaming to relax. The weeds can wait for a week, I can comfortably say no to requests for volunteering, and hey, nothing really bad happens if the laundry doesn't get put away until a day later.

Other generations may have different challenges, and they may need to let go of other parts of their lives in order to have the life they want. Maybe two hours of video gaming instead of four. Maybe we have to make studying our English Lit a priority this year. It's all about **focusing on what we need to focus on now**, getting it done, and moving on the job of living our lives fully and with passion.

The skills described in this book are just that—skills. They are not magic incantations, and will not fundamentally change how you view the world. However, how and if you use them will depend on what it is you want out of life, and that requires deep (and ongoing) inner reflection. If you *really* are content to live in chaos or constant stress, then no amount of skills will change that. But if you want a different path—one where you can do more with your time—then these skills will give you the tools you need to do just that.

As a closing to this book, I invite you to use the charts on the following pages—write down what you have learned about yourself, where you trip yourself up, and then write down how you are going to change these things, and live mindfully in a place of more productivity, less chaos, and most importantly more time to live and enjoy your life.

This is your life, your one shot. Make the **most** of it!

Time Management Worksheet

Flip back to the chapter on Time Management for review, and review your *Time Management Profile*. Make notes here about what you have learned, and what you still need to work on, with regards to this skill set.

What I know:	
Best time of day for work	
Ways I can regain focus	
How I know I need a break	
How I can use technology to manage my time	

What my pitfalls are:	
My biggest time-waster	
My biggest distraction	
Why I procrastinate	

What I can do to improve:	
Procrastination	
Distraction	
Letting go	

What is my relationship with time, and how do I want to improve it?

What is ONE THING I will do today to improve my relationship with time?

Space Management Worksheet

Review your notes in *Space Management*, and your answers in the worksheet at the end of that chapter. Then, answer the questions or make notes below.

What I know:	
Where I can put my 'most lost' items	
Why it's important where I put things	
How I can declutter	

What my pitfalls are:	
What I never put away	
What I don't have a place for	
Why I lose things	

What I can do to improve:	
Sorting/storing	
Keeping track of things	
Cleaning up	

What is my relationship with my space, and how do I want to improve it?

What is ONE THING I will do today to improve my relationship with my room or office?

Virtual Management Worksheet

Review your notes in *Virtual Management*, and your answers in the worksheet at the end of that chapter. Then, answer the questions or make notes below.

What I know:	
How I can use placement	
How I can use color	
How I can use symbols	
What my pitfalls are:	
What my file system looks like	
What I can never find	
Why I never organize	
What I can do to improve:	
Sorting/storing	
Keeping track of things	
Cleaning up	

What is my relationship with my virtual space, and how do I want to improve it?

What is ONE THING I will do today to improve my relationship with my virtual space?

Memory Management Worksheet

Review your notes in *Memory Management*, and your answers in the worksheet at the end of that chapter. Then, answer the questions or make notes below.

What I know:	
How I can write things down	
How I can set alarms	
How I can use multi-modal learning	
Why practice and repetition are important	
What my pitfalls are:	
Not understanding how I learn best	
Using only one method to study	
Not focusing on *learning*	
What I can do to improve:	
Multi-modality	
Alarms/scaffolds	
Manipulate/practice	

What is my relationship with my memory, and how do I want to improve it?

What is ONE THING I will do today to improve my relationship with my memory?

Project Management Worksheet

Review your notes in *Project Management*, and your answers in the worksheet at the end of that chapter. Then, answer the questions or make notes below.

What I know:	
Why I need a mission statement	
How to break down my mission into actual tasks	
Why it's important that they are SMART	
What my pitfalls are:	
Not taking the time to plan	
Resisting commitment	
Not sticking to it	
What I can do to improve:	
Unclear mission/goals	
Planning	
Increase motivation	

What is my relationship with managing projects, and how do I want to improve it?

What is ONE THING I will do today to improve my relationship with project management?

Information Management Worksheet

Review your notes in *Information Management*, and your answers in the worksheet at the end of that chapter. Then, answer the questions or make notes below.

What I know:	
Why *importance to task* is important	
Why *relatedness to task* is important	
Why *validity to task* is important	

What my pitfalls are:	
Not evaluating/ranking options effectively	
Not considering resources (time/resources/quality)	
Losing sight of the task at hand	

What I can do to improve:	
'Think through' all aspects of the mission/goals/tasks	
Pay attention to resources needed	
Pay attention to sequence and dependency	

What is my relationship with information management, and how do I want to improve it?

What is ONE THING I will do today to improve my relationship with information?

Thought Management Worksheet

Review your notes in *Thought Management*, and your answers in the worksheet at the end of that chapter. Then, answer the questions or make notes below.

What I know:	
I can use thought cessation and screening by	
I can use thought running and sorting when	
I can be more mindful of my thoughts by	
What my pitfalls are:	
Distorted thoughts	
Getting stuck in negativity	
Fearing change	
What I can do to improve:	
Question my distorted thoughts	
Proactively use thought cessation and screening	
Use mindfulness	

What is my relationship with my thoughts, and how do I want to improve it?

What is ONE THING I will do today to improve my relationship with my thoughts?

Obstacle Management Worksheet

Review your notes in *Obstacle Management*, and your answers in the worksheet at the end of that chapter. Then, answer the questions or make notes below.

What I know:	
I can plan for some obstacles	
When to reframe	
When to start over	
When to give up	

What my pitfalls are:	
Fear of failure	
Lack of motivation	
Anger at change	
Other	

What I can do to improve:	
Plan	
Let Go	
Self-care	

What is my relationship with obstacles, and how do I want to improve it?

What is ONE THING I will do today to improve my relationship with obstacles?

My Self-Affirmation

As your last exercise in this book, take the time to reflect on what you now know about yourself—both good and in need of improvement—and translate that into your personal self-affirmation.

Start by copying over the eight 'ONE THING' statements from all of the previous pages in this chapter here:

1.

2.

3.

4.

5.

6.

7.

8.

Next, read through these statements. Is there a theme? Do they work together to create a whole, or are there several individual thoughts? Either way, pick the ones that are most meaningful to you now, at this point in your life, and see if you can come up with one statement that you can tape to your monitor, post on your refrigerator, put on your Facebook status, that captures what you want to do with your life right now.

Then, turn the page.

I will become the CEO of myself by:

And make it so!

References

The following is a list of referential material used in the writing of this book.

The American Heritage® Medical Dictionary Copyright © 2007, 2004 by Houghton Mifflin Company. Published by *Houghton Mifflin Company*. Accessed online from Freeonline Dictionary, February 21, 2012. http://medical-dictionary. thefreedictionary.com/executive+function.

American Psychiatric Association. (2013). Diagnostic and statistical manual of mental disorders (5th ed.). Arlington, VA: American Psychiatric Publishing. pp. 155-188.

Ayres, I. (2010). *Carrots and Sticks: Unlock the power of incentives to get things done*. Bantam Books, New York, NY, pp. 28.

R. Barkley (2000). Excerpts from Lecture in San Francisco, June 17, 2000, published by permission by SchwabLearning.org, Charles and Helen Schwab Foundation, pp. 25.

Boch, F. & Piolat, A. (2005). Note taking and learning: a summary of research. *The WAC Journal,* Vol. 16: September 2005. pp. 101-113.

Brown, T. (2001). *Brown Attention-Deficit Disorder Scales®* [Measurement instrument]. Pearson Publishing, San Antonio, TX.

Bureau of Labor and Statistics. Productivity change in the nonfarm business sector, 1947-2011. Average annual percent change. http://www.bls.gov/lpc/prodybar. htm, retrieved February 8, 2012.

Burns, D. (1980). *Feeling Good: The New Mood Therapy.* HarperCollins, New York, NY.

The Real Reasons You're Working So Hard... and what you can do about it. Businessweek, October 3, 2005. Retrieved February 8, 2012.

Cahill, L., and McGaugh, JL. (1998). Mechanisms of emotional arousal and lasting declarative memory. *Trends in Neuroscience.* Jul; 21(7):249-9.

Chan, R. C. K., Shum, D., Toulopoulou, T. and Chen, E. Y. H. (2008). Assessment of executive functions: Review of instruments and identification of critical issues. *Archives of Clinical Neuropsychology.* 2 23 (2): 201-216.

Cooper-Kahn, J. and Dietzel, L. (2008). *Late, Lost, and Unprepared.* Woodbine House, Bethesda, MD.

Darrah, C., Freeman, J., English-Lueck, J. (2007). *Busier than ever! Why American families can't slow down.* Stanford University Press, Stanford, CA, pp. 248-249.

Dehaene, S., et al. (2006). Conscious, preconscious, and subliminal processing: A testable taxonomy. Trends in Cognitive Science. Vol 10(5): 204-11.

Dweck, C. and Leggett, E. (1988). A social-cognitive approach to motivation and personality. *Psychological Review,* Vol. 95(2), 256-273.

Erickson, M. and Reder, M. (1998). The effects of multiple repetitions on implicit memory across long durations. Department of Psychology, Carnegie Mellon University, Pittsburgh, PA. Unpublished manuscript.

Fadel, C. (2008). *Multimodal Learning Through Media: What the Research Says.* San Jose, CA: Cisco Systems. pp. 16.

Gladwell, M. (2005). *Blink.* Little, Brown and Company, New York, NY. pp. 32.

Herz, R. (2005). Odor-associative Learning and Emotion: Effects on Perception and Behavior, *Chemical Senses*, 30 (suppl 1): i250-i251.

Hill, Elisabeth L. (2004). Executive dysfunction in autism. *Trends in Cognitive Sciences,* 8 (1), pp. 26-32.

Hinshaw, S. P. and R. Scheffler (2014). The ADHD Explosion: Myths, Medication, Money, and Today's Push for Performance. Oxford University Press, New York, NY. pp. 31.

http://www.closetsdaily.com/closet-news/closets-industry-news/rubbermaid_survey_shows_clutter_leads_to_stress_129230503.html, accessed February 19, 2012.

V. Kalnikaite and S. Whittaker (2007). Does Taking Notes Help You Remember Better? *Exploring How Note Taking Relates to Memory.* Presented September 4, 2007, at the British HCI conference, Lancaster, UK.

C. Koch, N. Tsuchiya (2006). Attention and consciousness: two distinct brain processes. *Trends in Cognitive Sciences*, 11 (1), pp. 16-22.

Logie, R. (1995). *Visuo-spatial Working Memory*. Lawrence Erlbaum Associates, Hillsdale, AZ, pp. 64-92.

McGonigal, J. (2011). Reality is broken: Why games make us better and how they can change the world. The Penguin Press, New York, NY, pp. 186.

Miller, G. (1956). The magical number seven, plus or minus two: Some limits on our capacity for processing information. *The Psychological Review*, 1956, vol. 63, pp. 81-97.

Pabilonia, S. and L. Eldridge (2010). Bringing work home: Implications for BLS productivity measures. *Monthly Labor Review*, 133 (12), pp. 18-35.

Olafson, L., Schraw, G., Wadkins, T. (2007). Doing the things we do: A grounded theory of academic procrastination. *Journal of Educational Psychology*, Vol 99, No. 1, (12-25).

E. Ophir, C. Nass, and AD. Wagner (2009). Cognitive control in media multitaskers. Proceedings of the National Academy of Sciences, PNAS August 24, 2009; published online before print www.pnas.org_cgi_doi_10.1073_pnas.0903620106; accessed January 25th, 2012.

Rones, Philip L., Randy E. Ilg, and Jennifer M. Gardner (1997). Trends in hours of work since the mid-1970's. *Monthly Labor Review* April: 3- 14.

Shah, P., & Freedman, E. G. (2003). Visuospatial cognition in electronic learning. *Journal of Educational Computing Research*, 29(3), 315-324.

Shapira, N., et al. (2003). Problematic Internet Use: Proposed Classification and Diagnostic Criteria. *Depression and Anxiety Journal,* pp. 17:207–216.

Tan, D., Stefanucci, J., Proffitt, D. and Pausch, R. (2001). The infocockpit: Providing location and place to aid human memory. Proceedings of the 2001 *Workshop on Perceptive User Interfaces.* Published by ACM, New York, NY, 2001. Pp. 1-4.

van Reekum R, Stuss DT, and Ostrander L. (2005). Apathy: why care? *Journal of Neuropsychiatry & Clinical Neurosciences,* 17, pp. 7-19.

Varendi, H., Christensson, K., Porter, H., Winberg, J. (1997). Soothing effect of amniotic fluid smell in newborn infants. *Early Human Development* 51: 47-55.

M. Weiss, L. Trokenberg Hechtman, and G. Weiss (1999). ADHD in adulthood: A guide to current theory, diagnosis, and treatment. The John Hopkins University Press, Baltimore, Maryland, pp. 52.

C. Williams (2010). Incidental and intentional visual memory: What memories are and are not affected by encoding tasks? *Visual Cognition,* 18 (9), pp. 1348-1367.

Appendix

We've included a few more pieces of information for you here in the appendix to supplement the rest of this book. Some of this information is repeated from other sections in the book, but is presented here again for ease of use:

❑ **School Cheats**—information on aides, accommodations, and ideas that can help students in middle and high school, and in college.

❑ **Sleep Cheats**—information on sleep hygiene, ways to manage sleep hygiene, and general tricks to getting a good nights' sleep.

❑ **Ode to a Cell Phone**—ways that you can use your trusty cell phone to help you manage your life.

❑ **Cool Stuff**—a series of websites that you can check out for more ideas and information.

School Cheats

Many of the people reading this book either have ADHD themselves, have a child with it, or know another school-aged child with it. Here is a list of things you can do and accommodations you can use at home or ask your school to provide, either informally, or as part of a 504 plan, designed to help the student in school:

Problem	Solution
Inattention	Manipulate a small fidget (worry stone, squeeze ball).
	Be allowed to get up and walk to back of class.
	Be allowed to suck on very sour candy (Warheads).
	Sit at the front of the classroom.
	Be 'cued' by the teacher with an auditory rap on chalk-board.
	Listen to music or sound with one earbud at low level.
Fidgeting	Manipulate a small fidget (worry stone, squeeze ball).
	Be allowed to get up and walk to back of class.
	Be allowed to do a lap around the field.
	Be allowed to doodle.
Forgetting to write down assignments	Use cell phone to take picture of assignments on board.
	Be given time in class to use electronic calendar on cell phone to record all upcoming assignments.
Forgetting to turn in assignments	Set alarm on cell phone, kept on vibrate in front pocket, to two minutes after class starts to cue to turn in work.
Notes incomplete	Be allowed to use a LiveScribe pen to take notes and record lecture for later studying.
Difficulty doing homework	Eat a protein-rich snack after school or class.
	Sip ice-cold water.
	Set a timer for 20-30 minutes. Work for that period, then take a 5-minute stretch break. Reset timer and repeat.
	Do homework in an area that is relatively quiet, but where people can see your progress—kitchen table or library.
	Turn off all electronics.
	Take an exercise break—jump on a trampoline, run around the block, take the dog for a walk.

Sleep Cheats

Teens and young adults in particular can run into sleep problems, in large part because the 'adolescent brain' seems to be somewhat nocturnal, driving them to stay up late. Unfortunately, most schools start early in the morning, which plays havoc with the sleep cycle. Try some of these solutions:

Problem	Solution
Can't fall asleep	No caffeine after 2 pm, earlier if you are highly sensitive to it. This includes energy drinks and chocolate.
	No strenuous exercise within 2 hours of bedtime.
	Turn down the brightness on all electronics after 8 pm to lowest setting.
	Listen to mellow music or quiet radio talk show at a low level while falling asleep.
	Listen to white, pink, or brown noise while falling asleep.
	Use guided imagery exercises to relax.
	Avoid alcohol and marijuana.
Can't wake up	Set 'gentle' bedside alarm to fifteen minutes prior to your must get up time. Set 'obnoxious' alarm, across the room, to the must get up time. Over a period of time, you will learn to wake up to the 'gentle' alarm, rather than having to bolt across the room to turn off the obnoxious one!
	Once awake, do not go back to sleep. Take a lukewarm shower instead.
Sleep cycle dysregulated	Five consecutive days a week, get up at the same time, using the suggestions above. Do not take naps, and on weekends, do not sleep in later than additional two hours each day. Over time, you will be tired and ready for bed at an appropriate hour.
Sleepy	If your sleep is not otherwise dysregulated, take a 30-90 minute nap. Set an alarm if you need to.
	Take a brisk walk. Frequently, we get sleepy from not breathing deeply while sitting at a desk.
	If not overly sensitive, use a mild stimulant such as coffee.

Ode to a Cell Phone

Your cell phone is a wonderful tool and can help you be and stay organized. Check out some of these ideas below:

Tool	Use
Calendar	Nearly all cell phones have a calendar app, and many allow you to sync with an online calendar. This allows you to both enter new appointments on the go, but also can remind you of where you need to be next, and when to leave. Don't forget to add in a reminder that gives you enough time to get to your appointment.
Alarms/Reminders	Use the alarm feature on your cell phone to remind you to do things, like turn in homework, call the dentist, go to school, get up, feed the dog—whatever you tend to forget.
Task Lists	Keep a running task list of all of the outstanding things you need to do. If it's a long list, consider creating several lists, divided by category: different classes, home and work, long term and short term, and so forth. Check your list every morning to remind yourself of what you need to be working on.
Camera	Besides taking selfies, you can use your cell phone's camera to take pictures of things you want to remember—like the class assignment on the board, an example project for art, and so forth.
MP3 Player	Most of us know we can listen to music on our cellphones, but you can also download relaxation exercises, soothing sounds, and other stress-reducers to listen to.
Voice Recorder	If you have trouble remembering what you hear, or if you want to leave a quick verbal reminder to listen to later, download a recording app to your cell phone and record away.
Accelerometer	While you don't use this directly, you can download apps like Sleep for Android that uses the accelerometer in your phone to record your movements while sleeping. This then gives you a picture of your REM cycles and overall sleep health.

Cool Stuff

Some random, some useful, all interesting. If you have more, send them to us, and we'll try to add them when we revise the book!

Websites

- ❏ www.simplynoise.com—a gentle noise generator.
- ❏ www.chorewars.com—a wicked-fun game to get family chores done.
- ❏ www.stickk.com—a site to make incentive bets to help you stick to your goals.
- ❏ www.ohdontforget.com—a task reminder that sends you texts.
- ❏ www.rememberthemilk.com—a general task reminder.

Apps

- ❏ iTrackMood—allows you to track your mood, and send notes to your therapist.
- ❏ Any.do—great app to track to-do lists.
- ❏ Asana—a more powerful tool, allows you to track projects.
- ❏ Dexteria—this is a cool little app that helps increase fine motor skills while playing games.

Stuff

- ❏ Snuznluz—an alarm clock that makes payments to organization you hate most when you don't get up on time.
- ❏ LiveScribe pens—high-tech pens that audiorecord and create a searchable PDF of your handwritten notes.
- ❏ Reading guides—transparent colored guides that help focus on one word or line of text at a time.
- ❏ Highlighter tape—great for when you don't want to mark up a book, but need to highlight key phrases.
- ❏ Removable tab organizers—as above, to be used instead of 'dog-earring' pages.

THE CEO OF SELF

Made in the USA
Middletown, DE
21 August 2024

59507465R00113